Praise for *On the Fringes*

This beautifully crafted book has a heart. A heart which is driven by the need to get the best available support and help for the most important people in our schools: the children and young people we teach.

In *On the Fringes*, Jackie Ward creates an immersive environment for us to understand the common challenges and frustrations met by pupils, parents and teachers in the complex world of SEN. The thorough research which Jackie shares in the book helps illustrate the many underlying issues within our education system and culture, and this is to be highly commended.

On the Fringes is for any teacher, parent or educationalist alike – you will not be able to put it down. It's a personal perspective as well as a professional reflection on what we need to do in order to ensure that every child in every school has their individual needs met to the best of our ability.

Thank you, Jackie, for a thoroughly enjoyable learning journey.

**Nina Jackson, author, award-winning speaker,
mental health ambassador and
education consultant, Teach Learn Create Ltd**

On the Fringes is a book into which you are drawn right from the outset, as it begins with a real-life, personal account of what inspired the author to write it.

Packed with useful tips and advice, this solution-focused resource delves into why some groups are more vulnerable to exclusion than others, with a specific focus on those children and young people who have significant undiagnosed needs and complex mental health difficulties.

Jackie paints a detailed picture of the alternative education provision offered in a PRU setting and describes the components of a caring, nurturing approach designed to develop pupils' self-esteem and self-confidence. She also emphasises the paramount importance of early intervention and its value in curtailing the progress of challenging behaviours, and discusses the need for staff to develop empathy and emotional resilience in order to best help vulnerable children and young people.

To close the book, Jackie provides a ten-point manifesto on how the exclusion of children and young people can be prevented so that a better future is made possible for those who would otherwise be left on the fringes.

Cherryl Drabble, author and Assistant Head Teacher, Highfurlong School

I could provide so many stories to support this very important book. Jackie Ward rightly reminds us that the children who need love the most will ask for it in the most unusual ways. As a consequence, schools need to seek unusual ways to teach such young people. I use those words deliberately: schools and teachers are paid to teach children, not to stand them in corridors, sit them in isolation booths or send them out on the streets. However, high-stakes testing – coupled with high-stakes accountability – has led to some schools using hostile, reactive strategies with those children who often have quite specific social and emotional needs. *On the Fringes* rightly suggests that there is another way – based around more creative and proactive child-friendly strategies that allow every child to feel that they can succeed.

Will Ryan, education consultant and former assistant head of school effectiveness and Excellence in Cities coordinator, Rotherham Borough Council

Jackie Ward

On the Fringes

Preventing exclusion in schools through
inclusive, child-centred, needs-based practice

Crown House Publishing Limited
www.crownhouse.co.uk

First published by

Crown House Publishing Ltd
Crown Buildings,
Bancyfelin,
Carmarthen,
Wales, SA33 5ND, UK

www.crownhouse.co.uk

and

Crown House Publishing Company LLC
PO Box 2223,
Williston, VT 05495, USA

www.crownhousepublishing.com

Page 38, extract © Tirraoro, Tania (2017). Ofsted and CQC Report on One Year of SEND Inspections. It Isn't Pretty, *Special Needs Jungle* [blog] (19 October). Available at: https://specialneedsjungle.com/ofsted-and-cqc-report-on-one-year-of-send-inspections-it-isnt-pretty/. Used with kind permission of *Special Needs Jungle*. Pages 51–52, extracts © Ryan, Claire (2016). *That Kid*, *The Life of a Colourful SEND Family* [blog] (28 May). Available at: https://claireyr123.wordpress.com/2016/05/28/that-kid/. Used with kind permission. Pages 71, 72, extracts © *Special Needs Jungle*. Blower, Renata (2017). Is There Meaningful Accountability for Illegal Exclusions?, *Special Needs Jungle* [blog] (20 November). Available at: https://specialneedsjungle.com/is-there-meaningful-accountability-for-illegal-exclusions/. Used with kind permission. Pages 108–109, extracts © Com Res (2017). *Teacher Poll on Perceptions of ADHD: Findings* (London: MHP). Available at: https://www.adhdfoundation.org.uk/wp-content/uploads/2017/10/Teacher-Poll-on-ADHD-Findings-Oct-2018.pdf. Used with kind permission of the ADHD Foundation. The six principles of nurture on p. 124 are © The Nurture Group Network and are used with kind permission. Pages 128–129, extract © Schoolwell (2017). Schoolwell Exclusive Interview with Tammie Prince, *Schoolwell* [blog] (29 October). Available at: http://schoolwell.co.uk/exclusive-interview-tammie-prince/. Used with kind permission.

Quotes from Ofsted documents used in this publication have been approved under an Open Government Licence. Please visit http://www.nationalarchives.gov.uk/doc/open-government-licence/version/3/.

British Library of Cataloguing-in-Publication Data

A catalogue entry for this book is available from the British Library.

Print ISBN 978-178583351-9
Mobi ISBN 978-178583412-7
ePub ISBN 978-178583413-4
ePDF ISBN 978-178583414-1

LCCN 2018966184

Printed and bound in the UK by Gomer Press, Llandysul, Ceredigion

Acknowledgements

I would like to thank the following people for all their love, help and support in enabling me to write this book. It has been a long-held dream and ambition of mine to communicate my passionate beliefs and ideas about helping children and young people who are excluded from education and society.

First and foremost, my lovely husband, Andy, has been a constant source of inspiration and unconditional belief in my ability to write. He understands my daily travails and supports me every step of the way, although this book has impinged on our time together.

I would like to thank my Twitter – and now real-life – friends, Cherryl Drabble and Lynn McCann (both published, prolific authors), for spurring me on when it all felt too much!

Big thanks to my editor, Louise Penny, for tough love when I needed it; hopefully this is a better book for it!

And finally, thanks to all the lovely schools I have worked with, including my PRU, for the marvellous experiences, including the frustrations, which have informed this book.

Preface

An 8-year-old boy was the inspiration for writing this book. Permanently excluded from his mainstream primary school, he came to our pupil referral unit (PRU) where he stayed for about a year before moving on to a school for children with social, emotional and mental health (SEMH) difficulties. John was a 'naughty' boy who struggled to cope in the classroom. He loved playing with his friends but found it difficult when they did not do what he wanted them to. He was able to access learning, but only on his terms. If he felt thwarted he would scream and shout and lash out indiscriminately at both children and adults and it took him a long time to calm down. His teachers were becoming desperate as he would often destroy school property along the way. When John came to us, he initially settled well in a class of eight children, supported by at least two adults at any given time, but before long he started to display the behaviours which were so challenging for his mainstream school.

John was autistic. He had no formal diagnosis but it was clear to us that this lay at the heart of his difficulties. His need to control was part of his condition and he was having major sensory meltdowns when this did not happen. He had complex underlying needs and required a referral to the paediatric service for further investigation. This should have happened as soon as he started having difficulties, but it took until he arrived at the PRU. As deputy head and special educational needs coordinator (SENCO) it was my duty to ensure that the children in our care received appropriate help and support, and many of our children needed statementing and sometimes a placement in specialist provision. As a regular participant in edu-Twitter debates, I know that assigning 'labels' to children can be seen as controversial but I am a pragmatist; at this moment in time there is no way of getting pupils the help they need without one. An education, health and care plan (EHCP) (what was once called a statement) has to include evidence taken from medical and educational sources and no child can access additional funded help in mainstream or specialist provision without one.

However, I know that the biggest challenge we face is giving our vulnerable children the support and strategies they need to help them develop life skills. As a very wise teaching assistant (TA) from the PRU once said to a child who was rhyming off a long list of his diagnoses, 'No one will ever see these written on your back … you need to find a way to deal with them.' An excluded child, whatever their issues, certainly does *not* need a free pass to behaving badly and, in my opinion, we need to ensure that strategies for emotional regulation and self-management are firmly in place, as lacking these skills leaves them at a disadvantage – both now and, especially, as an adult.

John eventually settled in our PRU. Pupil numbers were small and the adults were skilled and able to give him strategies to cope in a world which was challenging for him. John was hypersensitive to noise – not if it emanated from him, however – and his sensory meltdowns were distressing, both for him and for the people around him. These became more infrequent, although it was plain that he would need a similar environment throughout his education in order to reach his full potential; a return to mainstream would not be the best thing for him. In the course of his time with us he got a diagnosis of autistic spectrum disorder (ASD), or autistic spectrum condition (ASC) as some prefer to call it, and as I will throughout this book. It is indeed a condition, and a lifelong one. He was then offered a place at the local SEMH school, with the support of an EHCP in place. PRUs are only intended to be used for short-term placements – we used to be referred to as a short-stay school, which I think is much better than saying a 'unit'. A unit sounds penal, whereas the term 'school' reminds us that the children are with us to carry on their education whilst learning how to manage their underlying conditions and behaviour.

Towards the end of the summer term in 2016, I was asked to deliver a workshop about exclusion at a local conference and I received permission to interview John and use his words in my presentation. I am afraid I broke down in tears at that point. I will be exploring his views in more detail later in this book but the words that haunt me most are the ones he wrote in my memory journal at the end of the year. I was taking early retirement from the PRU and setting up as an independent behaviour and special educational needs and disabilities (SEND) consultant as I wanted to work more closely with children in mainstream settings to prevent exclusion where possible. The children and staff wrote some lovely comments in the journal. John's said, 'hope you help children get back to mainstream school'. Cue more tears!

This book is my personal account of how a culture of exclusion is failing our young people, and how their lives are affected as a result. It is not meant to be an edu-research piece; I will leave that to those more qualified in the field than myself. I pride myself on being solution-focused, as a great head once inspired me to be, and I hope that in the course of this book I can inspire others with strategies to help some of our most vulnerable children, who can otherwise seem destined to remain on the fringes of society.

I do draw on facts or figures here; however, I am much more focused on real lives than dry data. Indeed, it is an emphasis on the latter that has sadly been the downfall of many of our young people. At the heart of this book lie human stories rather than statistics. I am also not setting out to make a particular political point as I've concluded that all governments tend do what is expedient for them, which is often also the cheapest option. My passion is for our children, and I want to help them as much as I possibly can – this book is dedicated to them.

Contents

Chapter 4: A view from the PRU: after the exclusion . 41

Chapter 5: The child: 'that kid' 51

Chapter 6: The parents' view 63

Chapter 7: Behaviour or complex need? 77

List of acronyms

ADHD – attention deficit hyperactivity disorder

ASC – autistic spectrum condition

ASD – autistic spectrum disorder

CAF – common assessment framework

CAMHS – child and adolescent mental health services

CYP – child/young person

EAL – English as an additional language

EHA – early help assessment

EHCP – education, health and care plan

EP – educational psychologist

EYFS – early years foundation stage

FSM – free school meals

HLTA – higher level teaching assistant

IBP – individual behaviour plan

IEP – individual education plan

LEA – local education authority

NAS – National Autistic Society

NEU – National Education Union

ODD – oppositional defiance disorder

OT – occupational therapy

PDA – pathological demand avoidance (a form of ASC)

PPA – planning, preparation and assessment (time given to teachers in the school day for this purpose)

PRU – pupil referral unit

PSHE – personal, social and health education

SALT – speech and language therapy

SATs – standard attainment tests

SEMH – social, emotional and mental health

SEN – special educational needs

SENCO – special educational needs coordinator

SEND – special educational needs and disabilities

SLCN – speech, language and communication needs

SPD – sensory processing disorder

SpLD – specific learning difficulty

TA – teaching assistant

TAF – team around the family

TESS – Traveller Education Support Services

Introduction

If I had to sum up my professional mantra, I'd say, 'Be solution-focused, but remember the children are not the problem.' Schools are faced with a harsh reality when attempting to access SEND provision, address behavioural issues and, ultimately, prevent exclusions. The system as it stands is beset with problems, but the children are not it. I know there are no easy answers but I do feel that much more can be done by individual schools to help the vulnerable children in their care and ensure that they are not on the fringes for life.

I came late to teaching – I was a mature student, beginning my degree course when my son was a baby and then following it up with a PGCE. My career commenced in pre-national curriculum days and teachers were basically allowed to choose what they did as long as they taught maths and English. In my early days of teaching, there was the freedom to cater for the individual and let them learn at a pace that was right for them.

Unless a child had a physical condition, special educational needs (SEN) were largely unrecognised in the way they are today – for instance, diagnoses of ASC and attention deficit hyperactivity disorder (ADHD), and concerns surrounding mental health, were far less common. There were special schools and schools for children with behavioural difficulties, but the processes for moving children into these were less formalised than they are now. Statements existed but few parents and teachers knew how to get them before they became enshrined in the 1981 Education Act.[1] Over the years, as procedures became more embedded in schools, there was much more inclusivity in mainstream and I feel I was a front-runner in terms of getting support for children who needed it via help from paediatric consultants and the statementing process.

Behaviour was similar to what it is now and, yes, there were disruptive children. However, I would argue that there was a greater expectation for teachers to 'manage' their classes, and I even encountered some heads who would tell new staff that it was their responsibility to sort out their classes. Exclusion was unheard of, although I did know of one child who spent some time in a specialist unit – this was before PRUs came into being in 1993 – until he was able to reintegrate back into school. It was only after the advent of Ofsted that heads started to look at whole-school behaviour policies and adopted the collective approach which is commonplace today.

I would suggest that schools have become far more prescriptive since I first started teaching, with a narrowing of the curriculum and of tolerance towards individual differences and needs. This is certainly part of the problem. I am not in possession of 'miracle cures' which solve every issue, but hope that I give a flavour of what *can* be done, despite the bureaucratic and financial obstacles which seem to stand in the way of success. I hope that schools will strengthen inclusive practices and have the confidence to employ strategies which contribute directly to a positive ethos with regard to SEN and exclusion. I will be referring to SEN throughout as these conditions can often be hidden, whereas disabilities are often more visible or evident.

I will be emphasising the many ways in which exclusion impacts on a child's self-esteem and life chances, leaving them on the margins of our society. I will detail how schools can be solution-focused in preventing this. However, before we look at these damaging effects, and ways to circumvent them, we first need to look at the mechanisms and systems as they stand. As such, I will begin with an analysis of the facts and figures to explore what is happening in schools, and by looking at the legalities of exclusions. As I've said, I think lived experiences say more than statistics can, so I'll be exploring exclusion from various points of view, drawing heavily on my experience within the system. Alongside this, I will examine exclusion procedures and the SEND Code of Practice in depth, to examine pre-emptive approaches. I will particularly be highlighting the role of early interventions in detecting underlying SEN and medical needs, as, in my experience, these are often at the core of the behaviours that lead to exclusion.

I hope to reach out to parents, educators and other concerned parties and implore them to look at a bigger picture, which has the child at its heart. We always need to remember that for every statistic, there is a real child whose future is at stake. Of crucial importance is the role of parents in minimising exclusions, as is listening to pupil voice – both are vital in helping schools to be solution-focused.

First and foremost, this book reflects my personal journey over 25 years of working with children, parents and schools. I draw on a rich seam of knowledge and experience in helping those on the fringes of education and society, and have seen what I am suggesting work. I am very passionate about helping children and young people but we need to understand the context in which that help takes place. We need to look at what came before and consider what may come after – in many ways this book is just the starting point for future debate.

Notes

1 See http://www.legislation.gov.uk/ukpga/1981/60/contents.

Chapter 1

Exclusion facts and figures

I'm not a fan of using data as the sole basis to make important decisions that affect children's lives, as it is too open to manipulation by decision-makers to suit their own ends. Figures can be massaged to fit just about any situation, often dependent on subjective opinion rather than dispassionate fact. Yet because we place collective trust in what data can tell us and use it to inform policy, it does have an impact on practice and, ultimately, people's lives. As Mike Schmoker says, 'Things get done only if the data we gather can inform and inspire those in a position to make a difference.'[1] So, whilst we must beware the limits of data as a measure of individual lived experience, we must also be aware of the ways in which it shapes decision-making, policy and, thus, children's lives.

What is the data on exclusions telling us?

Whilst this book is written from an unapologetically personal viewpoint, it is of course important to consider a certain amount of data in order to see the wider picture. In July 2017, the Department for Education published the previous year's annual figures for permanent and fixed-term exclusions in England. It came as no surprise to me that this revealed a steady upward trend. Rates of permanent exclusion across all state-funded primary, secondary and special schools rose from 0.07% in 2014–2015 to 0.08% in 2015–2016, whilst fixed-term exclusions rose from 3.88% to 4.29% in the same period.[2] The 2018 release reveals a rise to 0.10 and 4.76% respectively.[3] The jump in fixed-term exclusions is particularly concerning as this can be a signal that a school perceives its other options for managing behaviour have run out. Indeed, as the 2018 report says:

> Persistent disruptive behaviour remained the most common reason for permanent exclusions in state-funded primary, secondary and special schools – accounting for 2,755 (35.7 per cent) of all permanent exclusions in 2016/17.[4]

Commenting on trends in the data, the report notes:

> The groups that we usually expect to have higher rates are the ones that have increased exclusions since last year e.g. boys, pupils with special educational needs, pupils known to be eligible for and claiming free school meals and national curriculum years 9 and 10.[5]

There is something rather telling in the language of expectation here. The characteristics associated with higher rates of exclusion, quoted verbatim from the report, are as follows:

- Over half of all permanent (57.2 per cent) and fixed period (52.6 per cent) exclusions occur in national curriculum year 9 or above.

- A quarter (25.0 per cent) of all permanent exclusions were for pupils aged 14, and pupils of this age group also had the highest rate of fixed period exclusion, and the highest rate of pupils receiving one or more fixed period exclusion.

- The permanent exclusion rate for boys (0.15 per cent) was over three times higher than that for girls (0.04 per cent) and the fixed period exclusion rate was almost three times higher (6.91 compared with 2.53 per cent).

- Pupils known to be eligible for and claiming free school meals (FSM) had a permanent exclusion rate of 0.28 per cent and fixed period exclusion rate of 12.54 per cent – around four times higher than those who are not eligible (0.07 and 3.50 per cent respectively).

- Pupils known to be eligible for and claiming free school meals (FSM) accounted for 40.0 per cent of all permanent exclusions and 36.7 per cent of all fixed period exclusions.

- Pupils with identified special educational needs (SEN) accounted for around half of all permanent exclusions (46.7 per cent) and fixed period exclusions (44.9 per cent).

- Pupils with SEN support had the highest permanent exclusion rate at 0.35 per cent. This was six times higher than the rate for pupils with no SEN (0.06 per cent).

- Pupils with an Education, Health and Care (EHC) plan or with a statement of SEN had the highest fixed period exclusion rate at 15.93 per cent – over five times higher than pupils with no SEN (3.06 per cent).

- Pupils of Gypsy/Roma and Traveller of Irish Heritage ethnic groups had the highest rates of both permanent and fixed period exclusions, but as the population is relatively small these figures should be treated with some caution.

- Black Caribbean pupils had a permanent exclusion rate nearly three times higher (0.28 per cent) than the school population as a whole (0.10 per cent). Pupils of Asian ethnic groups had the lowest rates of permanent and fixed period exclusion.[6]

What does experience tell us?

Various conclusions could be drawn about why these groups are particularly vulnerable to exclusion, but I want to confine myself to a few pertinent observations from my own experience.

Primary-aged pupils

Recently, I have been seeing more and more exclusions of primary-aged pupils, and I fear that the balance will tip away from the concentration we currently see at Year 9 and above. Of course, all exclusions are hugely concerning, but exclusion at such a young age means that children are outside of mainstream education before their school lives have even really begun. I am especially concerned about the number of young children who are being permanently excluded, including multiple children from the same school. This is not to say that these schools are in the wrong – they are often desperate for help in dealing with disruptive, often violent, behaviour and are extremely concerned about the child's safety and the safety of other children and adults, as well as the disruption to learning and climate of anxiety that this can cause.

Boys

The statistics show that boys are more likely to be excluded than girls and, indeed, this was borne out at my PRU. We did, however, have girls who were excluded for extreme emotional reactions or physical assaults on other children and staff. They often needed intense one-to-one support and a referral either to child and adolescent mental health services (CAMHS) or the child psychology service, at which point it was finally recognised that many had ASC, sometimes including pathological demand avoidance (PDA). ASC is often more easily recognised in boys, as girls can be more adept at seeming to cope in social situations. Both boys and girls frequently displayed high anxiety, which manifested itself in their poor behaviour and was linked to home circumstances, social and communication difficulties, sensory issues and underlying medical needs, such as ASC and ADHD.

Children claiming free school meals

I have seen how socio-economic factors put children claiming free school meals (FSM) at more risk of exclusion, including difficulties in families accessing the right support at an early stage and/or an unwillingness to engage with children's social care, even when intervention is warranted. There is a dearth of expertise in some counties with regard to CAMHS and children's social care involvement, and this needs addressing if we are to seek a more cohesive approach from all agencies.

Perhaps the targeted use of pupil premium money needs to be rethought, if some groups are still very vulnerable and at a greater risk of exclusion than others. We also need to look at how funds are allocated to local education authorities (LEAs) with large numbers of exclusions and whether enough money is going to the schools who need it the most. Most of the heads I meet despair at how exclusion is linked to finite resources; often a modest sum would bring in much-needed help at an early stage, but the funds just aren't there.

Children with additional needs

When I taught in the PRU I was often outraged and indignant that so many children were coming to us with needs that hadn't been diagnosed in their mainstream setting. Now that I work with a range of primaries and secondaries, I can see just how desperately schools are struggling to get the right help: constrained by a lack of time, money and access to specialist knowledge and expertise. I will be exploring proactive strategies to help later in the book but, sadly, there is no magic wand. The help I offer in my professional practice often centres on getting children the right medical diagnosis and treatment, arranging an EHCP and finding the best provision to meet their needs. I've worked with a significant number of at-risk-of-exclusion children who appeared to have no discernible needs, which is to say that they didn't fit neatly into a statistical or diagnostic category. However, it soon became clear to me that these children had significant *undiagnosed* needs in terms of social communication, language or mental health difficulties. Again, I can only base this on my experience, but time and again, I've seen children being dismissed as 'naughty', and I have been instrumental in unpicking the underlying reasons for this behaviour. Understanding and meeting needs is a critical component of preventing exclusions, which will be returned to frequently in the following chapters.

I am extremely concerned by the statistically high exclusion rates for children with EHCPs. As I said in the introduction, there may be a problem, but the child isn't it. Once a child has a plan in place, they should be getting the support they need. A school should be calling an emergency review meeting to look again at the child's needs. If they are really struggling in mainstream, a special school may be deemed more appropriate, but exclusion is not the answer. We need to embed better systems for addressing and meeting needs, and employ appropriate strategies to pre-empt further difficulties – I will be offering suggestions later on in this book.

I am also very worried by the high exclusion rates for children receiving SEN support, and in my experience there are many more children who need this support but aren't getting access to it. Frequently there were children who arrived at the PRU who we deemed to be in need of SEN support, but rarely was there any evidence collated to explore these unmet needs. Unfortunately, behaviours are very visible, but needs are not; once behaviours reach crisis point, it is often too late to explore anything underlying. I am a great believer in early intervention, but if a child is on the verge of permanent exclusion then something needs to be done urgently. It is frustrating to see how other professionals, such as paediatricians, have to employ what seems like arbitrary guidance before they can further investigate or diagnose a condition. Whilst we are right to be cautious when it comes to labelling or medicating a child, I can't help but feel that the system isn't responsive enough in enabling schools and families to access support.

Children from Gypsy, Roma and Traveller backgrounds

The figures reveal that Gypsy, Roma and Traveller of Irish heritage children have the highest rate of both permanent and fixed-term exclusion. I've seen how hard county-level Traveller Education Support Services (TESS) work to engage families to combat non-attendance and to improve educational outcomes for those who do attend. In 2010 the Department for Children, Schools and Families commissioned a report on improving the outcomes for these pupils, which was published after it was renamed the Department for Education.[7] One key concern was that outcomes for secondary-aged pupils were in jeopardy as they rarely continued their education beyond the age of 14.

In my experience at the PRU, it was rare for parents from this background to support any form of secondary education, particularly when their children had been permanently excluded from mainstream provision. Even by Year 5 or 6, children were demonstrably disaffected with education. They also had a view that their education was about to end and that they would be starting employment with adult family males; often parents colluded in this, even when their child had the potential to do well academically. If parents withdrew their children, they would often say that this was to home educate them, even when they clearly did not have the capacity to do this. At the PRU, we tried to promote the value of education for Traveller communities, and we found the TESS inexhaustible in supporting parents, families and schools. However, there really needs to be a coordinated service at national level, rather than piecemeal regional strategies. This is particularly vital as children from Traveller communities can 'disappear' off the education radar by moving.

Some of the key findings of the review into the achievements of Gypsy, Roma and Traveller pupils were:

- Nationally, in both the primary and secondary phases, Gypsy, Roma and Traveller pupils have significantly higher levels of absence from school than pupils from other ethnic groups.[8]

- Without a framework of targeted support at both local and national levels, the improvement of outcomes for these pupils is likely to remain unacceptably slow.[9]

- The concentration of Gypsy, Roma and Traveller pupils in schools that achieve below average results needs to be addressed at strategic and policy levels. Future research could usefully examine the characteristics and educational experiences of high attaining pupils from these communities.[10]

- The maintenance of scripts can have a positive or limiting effect on outcomes. Developing relationships of trust through dialogue with families and community groups is important, so that community and parental scripts can be used as a way of opening positive discussion, rather than acting as a barrier to it.[11]

- Psycho-social factors are central to the question of raising outcomes. Schools need to fully recognise that, if Gypsy, Roma and Traveller pupils are unhappy in school, they are unlikely to attend or achieve.

Social difficulties may lead pupils to self-exclude or behave in a manner that results in exclusion.[12]

Again, high exclusion levels are still a problem. In my own experience, it is parental engagement that is the key to improving outcomes and reducing exclusion. Traveller services are indefatigable but they do not have magic wands. If most families are hit with fines for non-attendance and home-schooling is rigorously looked at, why are certain minority groups, in some instances, seemingly exempt from this? It may be that we don't want to be accused of causing racial or cultural offence, but I have seen academically bright children taken out of education at a young age because it is perceived as the 'norm' in their community. Why are we so blinkered when it comes to the welfare and wellbeing of these children? Our concern with cultural sensitivity may be adversely affecting the life chances of many young people.

Children from Black and minority ethnic (BAME) backgrounds

I am also fearful about the exclusion rates for certain ethnic groups. As long ago as 1985, Lord Swann reported at length on the concerns of the Black Caribbean community about the academic performance of their children: concerns about underachievement and vulnerability to exclusion from mainstream settings had been building in the preceding two decades.[13] The inquiry looked at the needs of pupils from all minority ethnic groups. Yet here we are, more than 30 years later, with the data on exclusions revealing that the same problems are still entrenched.

What is happening to excluded children?

Children excluded from mainstream education may be placed in a PRU. Figures for PRUs suggest:

The rate of permanent exclusion in pupil referral units decreased from 0.14 per cent in 2015/16 to 0.13 in 2016/17. After an increase from 2013/14 to 2014/15, permanent exclusions rates have remained fairly steady. [...] The fixed period exclusion rate has been steadily increasing since 2013/14.[14]

In my experience, permanent exclusions from a primary PRU are extremely rare but, statistically, exclusions are not unheard of in PRUs.

By virtue of temporary home education, many children are effectively kept 'out of the system' because alternative provision is not available immediately – something I experienced first-hand whilst at the PRU. For some, in the longer term, a move to specialist SEMH provision may be appropriate, although with early supportive interventions this may not become necessary.

One thing that really does concern me is the hidden number of 'grey' or illegal exclusions that are still prevalent in schools, as I will explore in greater detail in the next chapter. Heads may send children home to 'cool off' in the misguided belief they are helping them and their families by not issuing a fixed-period exclusion; however, this is merely hiding the problem rather than addressing the underlying issues – for example, SEN – which may need further investigation. It also means that if behaviour does then escalate, there is no paper trail to say what strategies (if any) were put in place or determine if a pattern is emerging. If a head then 'suddenly' decides to permanently exclude and a parent complains, the head could not necessarily count on the support of the governing body as due process wasn't followed. More significantly, this is breaking the law. The government has published clear guidelines for schools[15] and registered charities provide information for parents, including all the legalities of what can and cannot be done, as of September 2017, with regards to exclusion.[16] One wonders if these illegal exclusions had been recorded correctly whether the statistical picture for fixed-term exclusion would be even more bleak.

What are those in power doing about it?

In spring 2017, the government ran a five-week consultation on its exclusion guidance.[17] However, the emphasis was on clarifying areas that were causing confusion in the system rather than changing existing policy. Respondents – including schools, parents, LEAs, young people, unions and charities – argued that the guidance should insist that children's SEN be taken into account, but the Department for Education stated that was already made clear.[18] Similarly, it rejected the call for the guidance to be made more accessible to parents who do not speak English as a first language, claiming it was up to heads to make sure that these parents were fully informed.

So there we have it: a consultation which seems more concerned with tinkering around the edges of guidance than instigating real change, despite exclusion figures continuing to rise, with the most vulnerable groups being let down and left to the vagaries of limited budgets and provision. Children with SEN, children claiming FSM, children from minority backgrounds – what is the point of collecting statistics about their increased risk of exclusion if nothing more is to be done? Schmoker is spot on there. But let's not forget, behind the statistics lie real children, real families, with stories to tell. As Brené Brown posits, 'Maybe stories are just data with a soul.'[19]

Where is the soul in dry government statements which do not acknowledge that policy-makers have a duty to improve the life chances of future generations, including those on the fringes of society? Those children whose education and life chances are adversely impacted by exclusion, both from mainstream education and often mainstream life itself. They risk becoming marginalised for life if proper provision is not made for their education. It is often left to individuals, and to individual schools, to try to make a difference for our most vulnerable pupils, but the picture is so uneven it is almost a lottery as to which children receive help and which do not; this needs to change, but help is needed.

Notes

1 Michael J. Schmoker, *Results: The Key to Continuous School Improvement* (Alexandria, VA: Association for Supervision and Curriculum Development, 1996), p. 70.
2 Department for Education, Permanent and Fixed Period Exclusions in England: 2015 to 2016. SFR 35/2017 (20 July 2017). Available at: https://www.gov.uk/government/statistics/permanent-and-fixed-period-exclusions-in-england-2015-to-2016, p. 3.
3 Department for Education, Permanent and Fixed Period Exclusions in England: 2016 to 2017 (19 July 2018). Available at: https://www.gov.uk/government/statistics/permanent-and-fixed-period-exclusions-in-england-2016-to-2017, p. 3.
4 Department for Education, Permanent and Fixed Period Exclusions in England: 2016 to 2017, p. 5.
5 Department for Education, Permanent and Fixed Period Exclusions in England: 2016 to 2017, p. 6.
6 Department for Education, Permanent and Fixed Period Exclusions in England: 2016 to 2017, pp. 6–7.

7   Anne Wilkin et al., *Improving the Outcomes for Gypsy, Roma and Traveller Pupils: Final Report*, Research Report DFE-RR043 (London: Department for Education, 2010). Available at: https://www.gov.uk/government/publications/improving-the-outcomes-for-gypsy-roma-and-traveller-pupils-final-report.

8   Wilkin et al., *Improving the Outcomes for Gypsy, Roma and Traveller Pupils*, p. iii.

9   Wilkin et al., *Improving the Outcomes for Gypsy, Roma and Traveller Pupils*, p. 102.

10 Wilkin et al., *Improving the Outcomes for Gypsy, Roma and Traveller Pupils*, p. 102.

11 Wilkin et al., *Improving the Outcomes for Gypsy, Roma and Traveller Pupils*, p. x.

12 Wilkin et al., *Improving the Outcomes for Gypsy, Roma and Traveller Pupils*, p. xi.

13 Michael Swann (chairman), *Education for All: Report of the Committee of Enquiry into the Education of Children from Ethnic Minority Groups* [Swann Report] (London: Her Majesty's Stationery Office, 1985). Available at: http://www.educationengland.org.uk/documents/swann/swann1985.html.

14 Department for Education, Permanent and Fixed Period Exclusions in England: 2016 to 2017, p. 7.

15 Department for Education, *Exclusion from Maintained Schools, Academies and Pupil Referral Units in England: Statutory Guidance for Those with Legal Responsibilities in Relation to Exclusion*. Ref: DFE-00184-2017 (London: Department for Education, 2017). Available at: https://www.gov.uk/government/publications/school-exclusion.

16 See, for example, https://childawadvice.org.uk/.

17 Department for Education, *Exclusion Guidance 2017: Government Consultation*. Launch date: 14 March (London: Department for Education, 2017). Available at: https://consult.education.gov.uk/school-absence-and-exclusions-team/statutory-exclusion-guidance/.

18 Department for Education, *Exclusions from Maintained Schools, Academies and Pupil Referral Units in England: Government Consultation Response*. Ref: DFE-00183-2017 (London: Department for Education, 2017). Available at: http://dera.ioe.ac.uk/28702/11/Exclusion_Guidance_consultation_response.pdf, p. 5.

19 Brené Brown, The Power of Vulnerability [video], *TEDxHouston* (June 2010). Available at: https://www.ted.com/talks/brene_brown_on_vulnerability?language=en.

Chapter 2

The legalities of exclusion

Section 52 of the Education Act 2002 states that the head teacher of a maintained school may exclude a pupil from the school for a fixed period or permanently.[1] As briefly mentioned in Chapter 1, the Department for Education issues guidance for maintained schools, academies and PRUs to follow, which was updated in September 2017.[2]

Fixed-term exclusions

According to the Department for Education guidelines:

- A pupil may be excluded for one or more fixed periods (up to a maximum of 45 school days in a single academic year), or permanently. A fixed-period exclusion does not have to be for a continuous period.

- A fixed-period exclusion can also be for parts of the school day. For example, if a pupil's behaviour at lunchtime is disruptive, they may be excluded from the school premises for the duration of the lunchtime period. The legal requirements relating to exclusion, such as the head teacher's duty to notify parents, apply in all cases. Lunchtime exclusions are counted as half a school day for statistical purposes and in determining whether a governing board meeting is triggered.

- The law does not allow for extending a fixed-period exclusion or 'converting' a fixed-period exclusion into a permanent exclusion. In exceptional cases, usually where further evidence has come to light, a further fixed-period exclusion may be issued to begin immediately after the first period ends; or a permanent exclusion may be issued to begin immediately after the end of the fixed period.

- 'Informal' or 'unofficial' exclusions, such as sending a pupil home 'to cool off', are unlawful, regardless of whether they occur with the agreement of parents or carers. Any exclusion of a pupil, even for short periods of time, must be formally recorded.[3]

In what circumstances can a child be excluded?

A pupil must only be excluded on disciplinary grounds. The decision to exclude must be:

- lawful

- rational

- reasonable

- fair

- proportionate

Under the Equality Act 2010, schools must not discriminate against, harass or victimise pupils on the basis of:

- sex

- race

- disability

- religion or belief

- sexual orientation

- pregnancy or maternity

- gender reassignment

For disabled children, this includes a duty to make 'reasonable adjustments' to policies and practices and provide auxiliary aids.[4] Furthermore:

> It is unlawful to exclude for a non-disciplinary reason. For example, it would be unlawful to exclude a pupil simply because they have additional needs or a disability that the school feels it is unable to meet, or for a reason such as: academic attainment/ability; the action of a pupil's parents; or the failure of a pupil to meet specific conditions before they are reinstated, such as to attend a reintegration meeting. However, a pupil who repeatedly disobeys their teachers' academic instructions could, be subject to exclusion.[5]

Head teachers need to take into account their statutory duties when deciding whether to exclude a pupil. Formally arranged part-time timetables may be necessary as a temporary measure in exceptional circumstances to meet a pupil's needs, but must not be used as a disciplinary sanction or as a long-term solution.

However, the media is full of reports of exclusions which are not in line with this guidance. In September 2017, the *Birmingham Mail* reported that:

> a school in the North East has sparked headlines after parents claimed schoolchildren not wearing shoes an exact match to the uniform policy were being placed in isolation.[6]

Fifty pupils were put in isolation over the offence in one day. This is not an isolated incident. *Metro* reported in October 2017 that:

> an eight-year-old schoolboy has been threatened with exclusion if he doesn't remove his Sikh bangle while at school.[7]

I'm particularly saddened to hear of incidents that seek to sanction children's religious and cultural expression. Indeed, the Children's Commissioner's guidance on thresholds for exclusions is clear:

It is never appropriate to exclude for minor infringements of school rules, such as breaches of uniform rules or the wearing of jewellery, especially where such rules are more likely to disadvantage one gender, or certain ethnic groups, faiths or cultures.[8]

Exclusion is a serious business and the Children's Commissioner's guidance recommends:

The removal of a child from school premises by exclusion should only happen to:

- protect the health and safety of the individual; or
- protect the health and safety of others; or
- prevent disruption to learning.[9]

It's hard to see how these reported incidents fit into these principles.

Permanent exclusions

A decision to exclude permanently should only be taken:

- in response to a serious breach or persistent breaches of the school's behaviour policy; and

■ where allowing the pupil to remain in school would seriously harm the education or welfare of the pupil or others in school.[10]

Variations and grey areas

I just want to pause here and review these guidelines in light of my own experiences as a teacher, a PRU deputy head and an independent consultant. Most schools seek to follow the law to the letter, but what varies is the degree of tolerance shown to some pupils and the support available from professionals and the LEA. I would argue that *all* pupils facing exclusion should be investigated for underlying SEN, but if the LEA have limited resources it is hard for them to provide proper help for schools. I am often told by despairing head teachers, SENCOs and parents that they feel that they have been cut adrift by those who should be their first line of protection, and often money and lack of staffing are cited as the reasons for this.

There is another grave issue in terms of 'grey' exclusions. As I have mentioned previously, schools often exclude informally so that it will not impact adversely on children and families; however, as we heard from the Department for Education, informal or unofficial exclusions are unlawful. This is an area where rumour runs riot and some commentators allege that there are schools doing this on a regular basis, often at exam times, with the finger pointed at certain academies. Jarlath O'Brien, head teacher of Carwarden House Community School, has written an excellent and illuminating book, *Don't Send Him in Tomorrow*, which highlights this issue.[11]

My concern is that I do know schools that have used this approach, particularly with primary-aged children, to 'help' a situation without realising it is unlawful. If part-time education is put in place – which is allowable in certain situations – then the authorities must be consulted first, a risk assessment must be put in place, work must be sent home and the provision should be reviewed regularly with parents or carers. Often this is done to prevent permanent exclusion whilst consultation with other relevant professionals takes place; no school should go down this road without first liaising with the LEA.

It is interesting to read the Children's Commissioner's take on this:

These illegal exclusions are affecting a small, but we believe a significant minority of schools. We estimate that several hundred schools in England may be excluding children illegally, affecting thousands of children every year. This fact, surely, is a source of shame to the entire education system.[12]

At secondary level I am finding that schools often have their own internal provision for pupils with behavioural issues, but this varies from well-structured units which have strategies in place to help the pupil with self-regulation, to 'sin bins' where pupils with varying needs and challenging behaviour are all 'lumped together' with little regard for individual requirements. I also find that reduced timetables are prevalent, linked to what it is perceived that the student can 'cope' with.

I'm also concerned about the number of children 'missing' from the education system – for example, those simply refusing to attend. I know of one primary-aged child with two older brothers who had not attended secondary school for several years and just stayed around the house; their mother had resigned herself to this 'status quo'. This was some years ago, but it is not difficult to see how schools can get away with unlawful 'grey' exclusions.

Lastly I want to look at a school's obligations when a child has SEN or is 'looked after' by the LEA:

- There are certain groups of pupils with additional needs who are particularly vulnerable to the impacts of exclusion. This includes pupils with EHC plans and looked after children. The head teacher should, as far as possible, avoid permanently excluding any pupil with an EHC plan or a looked after child.

- Schools should engage proactively with parents in supporting the behaviour of pupils with additional needs. In relation to looked after children, schools should co-operate proactively with foster carers or children's home workers, the local authority that looks after the child and the local authority's virtual school head.

- Where a school has concerns about the behaviour, or risk of exclusion, of a child with additional needs, a pupil with an EHC plan or a looked after child, it should, in partnership with others (including the local authority as necessary), consider what additional support or alternative placement may be required. This should involve assessing the suitability of provision for a pupil's SEN. Where a pupil has an EHC plan, schools should consider requesting an early annual review or interim/emergency review.[13]

Looked-after children frequently came to the PRU because of their challenging needs, often as a result of undiagnosed SEN. Statemented children tended not to come to us as schools held emergency review meetings to sort out appropriate placements, yet Department for Education figures show that children with EHCPs are being permanently excluded, which is a dereliction of duty no matter how you dress it up.[14] An EHCP should protect children up to the age of 25 by ensuring they get the provision which meets their needs and is regularly reviewed. Financial support is provided for schools to cover additional support or specialised resources. Parental and child voice is an integral part of this process and the LEA has a statutory duty to adhere to the contents of EHCPs.

Notes

1   https://www.legislation.gov.uk/ukpga/2002/32/section/52.
2   Department for Education, *Exclusion from Maintained Schools.*
3   Department for Education, *Exclusion from Maintained Schools*, pp. 8–10.
4   Department for Education, *Exclusion from Maintained Schools*, p. 9.
5   Department for Education, *Exclusion from Maintained Schools*, pp. 9–10.
6   Kali Lindsay and James Rodger, The Shoes Sparking Controversy at School Where 150 Pupils Have Been Put in Isolation, *Birmingham Mail* (7 September 2017). Available at: https://www.birminghammail.co.uk/news/uk-news/shoes-sparking-controversy-school-150-13584251.
7   Oliver Wheaton, Boy Ordered to Remove Sikh Jewellery or Face Exclusion, *Metro* (2 October 2017). Available at: https://metro.co.uk/2017/10/02/boy-ordered-to-remove-sikh-jewellery-or-face-exclusion-6970656/.
8   Children's Commissioner, *'They Never Give up on You': School Exclusions Inquiry* (London: Office of the Children's Commissioner, 2012). Available at: https://www.childrenscommissioner.gov.uk/wp-content/uploads/2017/07/They-never-give-up-on-you-final-report.pdf, p. 21.
9   Children's Commissioner, *'They Never Give up on You'*, p. 21.
10 Department for Education, *Exclusion from Maintained Schools*, p. 10.
11 Jarlath O'Brien, *Don't Send Him in Tomorrow: Shining a Light on the Marginalised, Disenfranchised and Forgotten Children of Today's Schools* (Carmarthen: Independent Thinking Press, 2016).
12 Children's Commissioner, *'Always Someone Else's Problem': Office of the Children's Commissioner's Report on Illegal Exclusions* (London: Office of the Children's Commissioner, 2013). Available at: https://www.childrenscommissioner.gov.uk/wp-content/uploads/2017/07/Always_Someone_Elses_Problem.pdf, p. 4.
13 Department for Education, *Exclusion from Maintained Schools*, p. 11.
14 Department for Education, Permanent and Fixed Period Exclusions in England: 2016 to 2017, p. 7.

Chapter 3

The school's view: inclusion versus exclusion

Varying degrees of tolerance

The words of an anonymous teacher have become a well-known adage in education: 'The children who need love the most will ask for it in the most unloving ways.'[1] The sentiment expressed here is one we can recognise and empathise with, but how many 'unloving ways' can schools be expected to take? Is it fair for the rest of the class to be exposed to this and have their learning disrupted in the process? These are considerations schools have to take into account when faced with a disruptive child with challenging behaviours. The Department for Education guidance on exclusion is clear and detailed but it does not begin to address the emotional nuances surrounding such a monumental decision.

Teaching is certainly more standardised in approach and regulated by policy than it was when I first started. The question has to be, has this contributed to a 'zero tolerance' culture in some schools, particularly towards those children who have behavioural difficulties? I certainly see an immense variation from school to school in terms of what is deemed forgivable and what leads to immediate exclusion. I do wonder whether some primary settings are now too rigid to allow certain groups to function positively.

The Guardian reported on the increase in exclusions following the release of Department for Education statistics in 2017:

Commenting on the figures, Kevin Courtney, general secretary of the National Union of Teachers, said: 'This is a concerning trend and the DfE must give serious consideration to what is driving these rising numbers of exclusions.'[2]

He went on to highlight concerns about the narrowing curriculum, the culture of testing, and a reduction in the numbers of TAs.

We need to be creative about how we meet the needs of all learners and this includes broadening the curriculum and becoming more child-centred. From the second a child walks into class, there is not a moment of education to be lost, and teachers are held painfully accountable. Yet something arguably more precious is being lost: that instinctive knowledge on the part of the teacher that something is wrong or the chance for a child to talk about the weekend or share an achievement from home; that all-important relationship-building and bonding is being undermined. Often it is learning mentors or family support workers who liaise with parents, help with family crises, lend a listening ear or provide a shoulder to cry on. Whilst this is a great resource for schools, it can also mean that teachers are left unaware of important issues surrounding children in their class.

It is difficult to see how teachers can have any sort of pastoral input when this vital role is farmed out, 'leaving teachers to teach'. Building these relationships is essential; not some inconvenient part of school life which gets in the way of extra phonics or guided reading. To compound the problem at primary level, there is a proliferation of class interventions which occupy separate timetables with streamed groupings, meaning that teachers do not see their whole class as regularly. I am not against children receiving targeted support, but at what cost to their overall learning experience is this form of support provided? In secondary schools, pupils spend limited time with each of their teachers as they move from subject to subject. How can we build up a comprehensive picture of the whole child, their interests, strengths and weaknesses, if as teachers we hardly see them? And is it surprising that some children cannot cope with the demands of a busy classroom environment, either in accessing the curriculum or managing their own behaviour? The system is to blame for this; we are losing sight of our core purpose as teachers, in loco parentis. Parents, meanwhile, are working ever-longer hours – so some children are also missing out on the opportunity to spend meaningful time with the adults in their home lives.

Exclusion is not the solution

I have seen first-hand the effects of exclusion on children and families – for example, on John, the child discussed in the preface, and on distressed parents who feel inadequate. Removing the 'problem' from school is not the answer. Claire Wolstenholme and Nick Hodge say:

> It might initially feel like a relief when a pupil who is perceived as difficult and stressful is excluded from school. But exclusion can also leave many teachers with a sense of failure as they struggle with the unsettling question: 'Could I have done more?'[3]

Many of the teachers and heads I work with share this unease and try to exhaust all other sources of help and support, with exclusion coming as a last resort. Wolstenholme and Hodge go on to say:

> It is not difficult to see why so many exclusions occur. Schools find themselves trapped within what feel like competing government agendas: the mandate to include children and young people with SEND in mainstream; the ranking of schools according to pupil attainment; and the need to be seen to be strong on discipline and control.

Inclusion

Some schools appear to be more successful at inclusion than others. Why is this? And what do we mean by inclusion?

The Centre for Studies on Inclusive Education (CSIE) is an independent organisation set up in 1982 to actively support inclusive education as a human right of every child.[4] It has a wide remit, some of which I agree with – such as the support they provide to help schools be more inclusive –and some of which I do not – such as a commitment to the gradual closure of special schools, which they deem 'anachronistic'. Their website has many useful resources for promoting equality in schools. They do say that children have a right to an education in their locality – which is a tricky one in the current climate, as the National Education Union (NEU) says:

> Britain is facing the worst shortage of school places for decades. This is resulting in overcrowded classrooms, primary schools expanding beyond an optimum size and children travelling further to school.[5]

Many PRUs and special schools are not necessarily in a child's locality, so children may have to travel to access specialist provision. But is there an answer to the growing problem of regional mainstream place shortages? Kevin Courtney argued that:

> Government must return powers and funding to local authorities to enable them to plan and manage school places in a rational and cost-effective way.[6]

As funding is a massive issue across the whole of education, I do not feel that a solution will come any time soon. For some children, being educated outside their area can be stressful and difficult, but is often necessary for them to access the provision they need.

A study led by Mark Penfold that looked at pupils from new migrant Roma communities showed that inclusive policies work well, but only if they are targeted appropriately and well-resourced.[7] He says that one school in the north of England had reduced exclusions amongst this vulnerable group by offering support strategies:

- Strong support for our most vulnerable pupils is speedy and effective from our large Inclusion Team and Nurture Provision. Pupils who access this support show excellent improvement in behaviour, attitudes to learning and confidence. We have had zero exclusions for several years.

- There is a strong inclusion ethos that promotes equal opportunities and respect for each other. This is evident across the curriculum and in the many celebratory events such as international days, special assemblies, performances and community events.[8]

This proves what schools can achieve when they have the resources and focus. The report notes how the school has seen a 'rapid improvement in attendance' from the children, which has been achieved by staff ensuring that 'their diverse and significant needs' are met 'through classroom support and a wide range of interventions' – for example, language support and free breakfasts for pupils and their parents.[9]

The critical role of communication

Wolstenholme and Hodge's research suggests that regular positive communication with pupils and parents could reduce permanent exclusions.[10] My own experiences suggest that communication and talking are indeed key; however, the discussion needs to begin at the earliest possible stage, before difficulties become embedded. Emotion Works is an amazing programme for emotional learning and literacy which offers online training and a range of digital resources which are invaluable in my work as a specialist teacher of SEMH.[11] These often form part of primary and secondary school-wide practice in Scotland, where the enterprise was developed. One boy with anger management issues, who had come to the PRU in danger of permanent exclusion, responded really positively to regular discussions using Emotion Works materials. He is now in a mainstream Year 6 class and, whilst not perfect, has made really good progress. It helps that his current teacher has a great relationship with him.

The issue of communication can be particularly pertinent in the case of learners who speak English as an additional language (EAL). In some of the schools I work in there is good use of staff who speak community languages to ease transition and ensure that integration is speedy without negatively impacting on the child's cultural experiences.

In fact, my career began as an EAL support teacher in an infant school in which a significant proportion of pupils were of Pakistani heritage and spoke a first language other than English. Funding for such posts, which was ring-fenced in the 1980s, has since been subsumed into other budgets and some schools are relying more on bilingual support staff rather than specialists, if they can afford them. I am now seeing that some children with EAL and SEN are struggling to get the support they need, often resulting in them showing some challenging behaviours. This is particularly difficult for families who have little or no English themselves, as they have to rely on interpreters to access the right help from professionals.

Children with EAL often presented at the PRU with behavioural difficulties due to a language deficit, in their home language as well as English, and a range of undiagnosed needs. Poor social and communication skills led to them leaving mainstream education, either as a respite placement or as the result of permanent exclusion. Due to their challenging behaviours, we were seen as the 'right' provision. Usually the behaviours were down to the frustration they felt in their struggle to communicate: they were often confused and traumatised, sometimes having been thrust into a new country and a new school. We often felt that schools could be doing more to help these children before resorting to exclusion, although now I can see the pressures they were under.

Often, parents struggled to communicate – and this only compounded the issue. It was often difficult to persuade them to engage with relevant medical professionals through referrals and subsequent appointments; they needed high levels of support from school staff. However, if parents trust you and know you are there to help them and their children, they are more likely to meet you half way. One mother literally used to hide around the corner, refusing to come anywhere near school, but she is now actively engaged. The change came when a staff member, who spoke her first language, and I chatted with her informally in the parents' room rather than holding a formal meeting. We showed her examples of her child's work so she could see what he was doing well, not just what he struggled with. This positive interaction could then be built on.

If a child has EAL and SEN, parents are sometimes fortunate to receive home language support and can be accompanied to appointments by staff who can act as translators. This works well but is very intensive as often everything will need translating – discussions, reports, follow-up appointments and team around the family (TAF) meetings. Without this, the child is in danger of slipping through the net, particularly if they require the support of an EHCP. Some schools provide extra adult support, but some may not be able to afford this. Frustration and a lack of understanding result, whether this is down to language barriers or other blocks to effective communication. Again, we can see how variations in funding affect schools' ability to employ inclusion strategies.

In 2016, respected commentator Diane Leedham said:

EAL learners – that's one sixth of young people at school in England – remain invisible in the national conversation about education. [...] Teachers report high levels of anxiety about the lack of support and advice, but there is silence in the corridors of power.[12]

This is a damning indictment of what is happening at government level and it is no surprise that, in the absence of support, learners with EAL may face exclusion of one kind or another. However, if we are proactive and search for resources we can integrate into our practice, there is no reason why we cannot make a massive difference in helping learners with EAL and complex needs, rather than pushing the 'exclude' button.

A number of organisations have developed resources for schools to use to help EAL learners, often available for free or for a small fee. The Bell Foundation has created an EAL assessment framework which is free to schools, and can be used to support EAL learners at each stage of their language development.[13] EAL Nexus provides advice and fabulous resource packs which cater for beginner, intermediate and advanced learners.[14] The National Association for Language Development In the Curriculum (NALDIC) website also offers a host of useful resources for primary and secondary learners, which link to all areas of the curriculum.[15]

Characteristics of inclusive schools

What makes some schools more inclusive than others? I've observed some common characteristics:

- The leadership and management have embedded inclusive policies and practices.

- There is a good understanding of SEN issues and how to make appropriate provision.

- Pupils with behavioural issues are identified at an early stage and underlying medical needs are investigated.

- Appropriate support, tailored to a child's needs, is put in place at an early stage – for example, a child displaying signs of ASC may benefit from visual resources, such as a pictorial daily timetable, so that they are not anxious about what will happen next, which can lead to outbursts in class.

- They embrace differences and recognise when support is needed. They look at the needs of individual children and plan how best to meet those needs.

- They have the monetary resources to support children as appropriate. This could be in the form of extra staffing or physical resources to meet a range of needs – for example, a weighted blanket for a child who is hyposensitive to touch (sensory issues are often a cause of meltdowns if not appropriately catered for).

- The SENCO is proactive and able to initiate correct support procedures. They have access to outside advice and support to enable this – for example, specialist teachers, professional support services, SEN professionals from the LEA and a range of medical and mental health services.

- Parents and carers are fully included in monitoring and managing their child's needs.

- Professional support is accessed at an early stage – for example, a referral to a family doctor, paediatrician or CAMHS. SEN services in the LEA are able to signpost appropriate actions.

- High quality teaching is a feature of classroom practice with coordinated adult support as appropriate – for example, a TA or learning mentor working closely with the teacher in planning and carrying out next steps to support learners.

- Correct SEN procedures are in place when applying for an EHCP, and paperwork and evidencing is tight.

This is not to say that schools who do not display these characteristics are negligent, but rather that they need support. As an independent consultant, I often find that schools lack time and expertise to deliver the SEN agenda appropriately and they need help to manage this.

So what are the characteristics of schools excluding children? These vary; however, there are often some common denominators:

- Poor management or whole-school issues; often a new head or management team is called in to 'pick up the pieces'.

- High expectations of behaviour and zero tolerance for even minor infringements of the behaviour policy. A one-size-fits-all approach often does not take into account the varying needs of the children.

- A poor understanding of SEN, leading to an identification of 'naughty' behaviour rather than underlying need.

- Lacking external support from other relevant services – for example, early intervention teams and medical professionals.

- Lacking the financial resources to support needs due to budgetary constraints.

- Children are unable to access mainstream provision despite full support.

In my experience, schools in areas of deprivation with high pupil premium numbers often have more effective systems in place for managing challenging children than schools in 'leafy suburbs'. For instance, they may have their own nurture provision, usually in the form of a calming space in school with staff trained to provide specific interventions for children with social and emotional needs, as I explore fully in Chapter 10. A range of staff – for example, learning mentors, family support workers, social workers, counsellors, therapists and specialist teachers – are trained to support SEN and behavioural issues within the school community. This is not just the remit of the SENCO and management team but of all staff.

SEND provision in mainstream education

An essential characteristic of inclusive schools is a whole-school understanding of, and approach to, SEND; however, this is not widespread. Tania Tirraoro summarised a report by Ofsted and the Care Quality Commission (CQC) one year on from the revision of the SEND inspection frame-work. There were some disturbing findings:

School and area leaders did not have appropriate plans to deal with the levels of exclusion and had used unofficial exclusions too readily to cope with children and young people who have SEND. An 'alarming' number of parents said they'd been asked to take their children home. This was in addition, or as an alternative, to fixed-term exclusions. It is illegal.

Many parents of children or young people who have SEND reported concerns about the quality of staff training and teachers' ability to meet their child's specific needs when in mainstream school.[16]

It is so important to ensure that schools receive the right help and support to meet the needs of pupils with SEND, and avoid exclusions being used as a dubious, and illegal, short-term management strategy. Schools need to be proactive in finding out what support services are out there, whether in the LEA or independent. I would like to share the story of a very inspirational head who describes his school, in which 72% of pupils receive the pupil premium, as 'the most deprived primary in Leeds'. Chris Dyson is charismatic and, more importantly, passionate and committed to his school, Parklands, which has 300 pupils on roll and was rated 'inadequate' by Ofsted when he took up post.[17] Between 2013 and 2014 they had five different head teachers. Chris has been head teacher for four years and the school has recently been graded 'outstanding'. When Chris started, there had been 150 exclusions in the previous year, but they now have a zero-exclusions culture. So what has changed? Chris says:

> The staff needed empowering [...] the staff needed to feel part of a team. In short, the staff needed trusting and being believed in.[18]

Chris initiated a ban on shouting at pupils and created a new behaviour policy with input from staff, pupils and parents. Four years on, they have zero exclusions, and Ofsted could not find a single example of 'low level' disruption during their latest inspection.

> I believe in a 'can do' methodology. Smiles, love and respect can help pupils (and staff) throw off the shackles and be the best they can be.[19]

There are no 'magic bullets' and Chris still struggles within budgetary constraints. However, it is vital to have passion and belief in your vision of an inclusive school. I asked at the beginning of this chapter, how many 'unloving ways' can a school be expected to take? This will be down to the individual school but we need to be able to look at ourselves in the mirror and know that we did the right thing for that child, whatever the outcome.

Notes

1   Quoted in Russell A. Barkley, *Taking Charge of ADHD: The Complete,
    Authoritative Guide for Parents*, rev edn (New York: The Guilford Press,
    2000), p. 5.
2   Sally Weale and Pamela Duncan, Number of Children Expelled
    from English Schools Hits 35 a Day, *The Guardian* (20 July 2017).
    Available at: https://www.theguardian.com/education/2017/jul/20/
    number-children-expelled-english-schools.
3   Claire Wolstenholme and Nick Hodge, SEND Focus: 'Exclusion Affects
    Everyone – Pupils, Parents and Teachers', *TES* (14 June 2016).
    Available at: https://www.tes.com/news/send-focus-exclusion-affects-
    everyone-pupils-parents-and-teachers.
4   http://www.csie.org.uk/.
5   https://www.teachers.org.uk/edufacts/school-places-crisis.
6   NEU, Kevin Courtney, Joint General Secretary of the National Education
    Union, comments on plans announced today by Damian Hinds, the Secretary
    of State for Education [press release] (11 May 2018). Available at: https://neu.
    org.uk/latest/school-places.
7   Mark Penfold, *Improving Education Outcomes for Pupils from the New Roma
    Communities* (Leicester: EAL Nexus and the British Council, 2016). Available
    at: https://ealresources.bell-foundation.org.uk/sites/default/files/document-
    files/Improving%20education%20outcomes%20for%20Roma%20pupils.pdf.
8   Penfold, *Improving Education Outcomes*, p. 63.
9   Penfold, *Improving Education Outcomes*, p. 64.
10 Wolstenholme and Hodge, SEND Focus.
11 https://www.emotionworks.org.uk.
12 Diane Leedham, Nobody Puts EAL in the Corner, *Schools Week* (23 April
    2016). Available at: https://schoolsweek.co.uk/eal-learners-in-schools-
    how-the-government-could-help/.
13 https://www.bell-foundation.org.uk/eal-programme/.
14 https://ealresources.bell-foundation.org.uk/.
15 https://naldic.org.uk/.
16 Tania Tirraoro, Ofsted and CQC Report on One Year of SEND
    Inspections. It Isn't Pretty, *Special Needs Jungle* [blog] (19
    October 2017). Available at: https://specialneedsjungle.com/
    ofsted-and-cqc-report-on-one-year-of-send-inspections-it-isnt-pretty/.
17 Follow Chris on Twitter for more of the Parklands story. He is @chrisdysonHT.
18 Chris Dyson, This is What Teachers Need: Smiles and Love, *Integrity
    Coaching* [blog] (16 October 2017). Available at: https://www.
    integritycoaching.co.uk/blog/what-teachers-need.
19 Elizabeth Holmes, More Smiles, Less Stick: Chris Dyson on a
    Positive Approach to Behaviour, *Optimus Education* [blog] (29
    November 2017). Available at: http://blog.optimus-education.com
    more-smiles-less-stick-chris-dyson-positive-approach-behaviour.

Chapter 4

A view from the PRU: after the exclusion

The nature of PRU placements

When a child is permanently excluded they will usually be placed in a PRU or other suitable alternative provision. In my first years at the PRU we took lots of pupils who were at risk of permanent exclusion on respite placements. They remained on their school roll and we would regularly turn around their behaviour and successfully return them to their mainstream settings. However, over time, more and more children were presenting with complex needs and rarely went back to mainstream; instead they were being statemented and moving on to specialist provision. It is difficult to say why there was such a change – was it to do with an increase in SEN diagnoses? Was behaviour escalating to an unprecedented degree? Or was it that children were increasingly being expected to conform to a system that they just could not cope with? This third option links back to the point about varying levels of tolerance that I raised in the last chapter.

At our PRU, classes were small – up to eight pupils – with a teacher and TA in each. Children with severe needs had extra adult support both inside and outside the classroom. In my last year at the PRU all places were full and any subsequent pupils who needed a place had to stay at home, with tutoring from the LEA, until one became available. The tutoring would either take place in the home or in a local facility – for example, a library – for about an hour a day. Even though this service was limited, parents spoke highly of it as they felt that their children were accessing learning in a non-threatening environment for the first time. Sometimes, medical interventions – for example, ADHD diagnosis and treatment – would run alongside this and could be monitored more easily than in a mainstream setting.

Drawn to the most vulnerable

I am often asked what it is like to work in a PRU and how I came to teach there. I had taught for a number of years in a range of mainstream settings and was drawn to the most troubled, vulnerable children who struggled to cope with school life. In my second school there were many such children whose difficulties were linked to their home life or to underlying medical needs, such as ADHD (although this was not recognised then). I was seconded as a deputy head in a large school which had high numbers of pupils with SEN and challenging behaviours. The children were often volatile; however, I loved the job and the children and was fortunate to work for an amazing head teacher whose compassion and care for her pupils was limitless.

Part of my role entailed helping out in classes when children were unsettled and displaying inappropriate behaviours, and I would often talk to them afterwards to try to unpick what was going wrong for them. Usually, they just needed a safe space to retreat to and time to calm down and settle. They needed to build trust with a familiar adult and some time out to discuss their worries or just sit quietly until they were ready to rejoin the class. I knew then that I needed to do something different, and when I was offered a secondment to the PRU it felt like karma and I jumped at the chance. Some months later, I was lucky enough to become deputy head and I was delighted; I knew I had come home.

My first impressions were that this was just another school, albeit smaller, both in terms of the building and class sizes. It could take a maximum of 32 pupils at any one time. There was one Key Stage 1 class and the other three were Key Stage 2. Children were usually grouped according to age although there were exceptions according to nurture needs. It soon became apparent that the children had a range of difficulties and could go from being calm to extremely angry at a moment's notice.

Behaviour policy: rewards and sanctions

Once in the PRU the child would receive an education tailored to their needs. The personal, social and health education (PSHE) curriculum was vital in addressing the needs of disaffected and vulnerable young children from the ages of 5 to 11. PSHE shaped a nurturing curriculum and reinforced rules and boundaries. The behaviour policy was made very explicit to staff and children and was scaffolded by rewards and sanctions. There was a points system for all children in Key Stage 2: they earned points for behaving in each session, travelling well in the taxi or minibus, completing homework and so on. In Key Stage 1 the children had a chart which got stamped for good behaviour, kind words, trying hard with their work and so on. All children had playtime and lunchtime stickers and could earn small rewards at the end of the day or week. Staff addressed the children in the same way and there was a fair, calm, consistent approach across the whole school. When you have groups of volatile children all in one space you need structure and everyone singing from the same song sheet.

Sanctions were also in place. The atmosphere was overwhelmingly positive, but children needed to know that if they deliberately flouted the rules there would be consequences. They might have to make up time for lost learning or be separated from others if they were aggressive or damaged school property. In some cases – for example, the use of extreme violence – we would issue fixed-term exclusions. I have only known one instance of a permanent exclusion from a primary PRU and that was when a child brought a knife into school – staff and children need to be in a safe environment, just as in any school.

Structures and routines

The school day was very structured, beginning with the children arriving in taxis or minibuses with a passenger assistant to supervise their safety. A staff member would meet and greet to ensure that each child had a warm welcome; any issues that had transpired on the transport could be ironed out at this point. Many children travelled long distances and shared a vehicle with others, which could lead to disputes. Transport was provided by the LEA and was tightly risk assessed to ensure the safety of all concerned. Any incidents which jeopardised this could lead to either the parent having to accompany their child or the child being barred altogether, so these were swiftly resolved as parents often had no other means of getting their child to the PRU.

Breakfast was provided and this was a time for socialisation and for the adults to model good manners and appropriate conversation. In Key Stage 1 the children all sat round one table and had their own placemats, which they had designed and made. They would take it in turns to be the 'breakfast monitor' and help with buttering toast and putting out fruit. If breakfast went well the children could put tokens in a jar; when a certain number were collected the group could choose a 'special breakfast' which their teacher provided. This could be pancakes or even a cooked breakfast, and the children loved it. Positive rewards worked well but at the heart of our success was a nurturing approach and good relationships built up over time.

I have seen some mainstream schools use this nurturing approach really well, but often breakfast club is large and noisy, which is not helpful for children with SEN and behaviour issues. It would be beneficial for schools to accommodate a smaller group area for those who have sensory issues in relation to noise and crowds. Some schools have a 'lunch bunch' club for children who struggle in a large dining hall. Pupils sit with a familiar, trusted adult and also learn social skills, including good manners and appropriate ways of eating. One young girl with ADHD used to grab food with her hands and ignore others around the table, but now, with encouragement, she can use cutlery well and talk nicely to other children and adults; as a result she is more confident and has higher self-esteem.

Once in school, the children went to their classes and settled down with quiet, independent tasks such as reading and spelling or, in Key Stage 1, activities such as jigsaws. Any child who was not calm on arrival had the chance to discuss any problems or issues with a member of the behaviour support team before accessing class. This is a really good strategy for mainstream schools to adopt, with a teacher, support assistant or member of the pastoral team acting as a mentor. Giving a child space to talk or calm down is invaluable; much better than having them attempt to enter a classroom in an unsettled state, which often leads to disruption.

I have seen this work first-hand. In one secondary school, a young man with ASC needed to access a safe space before he entered class. His head of year agreed that he could use his office for this and could also take work there if he became agitated during a lesson. The pupil had a target for increasing the amount of time he spent in class, which he was working towards in small steps that he was 'in charge of'. I often find that children with ASC or ADHD need to have some form of control, which is carefully scaffolded by the adults to give an acceptable outcome. It is not about the pupil 'getting their own way' but about choices which suit both parties.

Playtimes and lunchtimes were structured with outdoor and indoor activities, well-supervised by adults as these were the times when disputes were most likely to occur. I often find that difficulties in mainstream schools happen at unstructured times. The judicious deployment of adults and/ or small, structured activity groups can have a positive effect on behaviour. One primary school I went into had a wonderful lunchtime staff member who had developed just the right approach with a Key Stage 1 child who was demonstrating challenging behaviours during these unstructured periods. She could spot early warning signs when the child was becoming unsettled and would take his hand and chat about something he enjoyed doing. We discovered he liked doing 'jobs' and so he got to look after the key to the shed where the playground equipment was stored and help tidy away at the end of the session. We then used an individual behaviour plan (IBP) to share these strategies with other staff.

PSHE ran through the curriculum and there were regular circle times and assemblies. There was an emphasis on sporting activities and each class accessed forest school on a weekly basis, which encouraged team-building, cooperation and resilience. Each child was encouraged to develop their strengths to build self-esteem and self-confidence, as when they first arrived these were sadly lacking. They often felt they had failed and were completely demoralised. They also had to come to terms with the things they found difficult; for many of our pupils this included writing, and underlying learning needs, including dyslexia, were prevalent. All of them struggled with behaviour, hence their placement in the PRU, and needed strategies to help manage this. Children with SEMH issues need a lot of modelling and positive reinforcement in order to make progress. Again this is something that mainstream schools could focus on through PSHE, providing positive models for behaviour with an emphasis on raising self-esteem and self-confidence.

I feel that the key to success in a mainstream setting is giving *all* pupils a chance to demonstrate their strengths rather than focus on their difficulties. They also need access to a broad and varied curriculum. In many schools PSHE has been squeezed out by the relentless focus on core subjects. Reading, writing and maths are certainly vital skills but the pendulum has swung so far that creative activities – such as art, music and design technology – are becoming rare in some primary schools from Year 1 onwards, whilst in secondary the emphasis is on success in key exam subjects.

SEMH awareness

The Telegraph reported on a NASUWT survey that revealed teachers' concern about anxiety, panic attacks and depression in young children; in one case an 8-year-old said he wanted to kill himself.[1] At our PRU mental health difficulties were common in pupils of all ages, and incidents of self-harm – such as head banging, intense scratching and attempts at self-strangulation – were on the increase by the time I left.

As well as SEMH needs, pupils often had unmet medical needs such as ADHD which needed addressing before strategies could be expected to make an impact; medication could be life-changing for our pupils. Staff receive training from a specialist company called Team-Teach, so they know how to react to violent children safely, including where violence is self-directed.[2] The approach uses a toolbox of positive strategies with the aim of maintaining a safe environment and reducing risk. Techniques for safe restraint are taught, but these are only to be used as a last resort; most of the training is about pre-empting and de-escalating situations.

Again, this comes down to having a positive relationship with a child who may be in crisis. A calm approach, maintaining rather than invading personal space and speaking calmly rather than shouting, will always help. In any setting, it is useful to share knowledge about effective individualised strategies amongst the adults working with a child via an IBP. Consistency is key and all adults – parents, teachers, support staff and welfare staff – should work together to decide on a course of action which will defuse rather than exacerbate a difficult situation.

Values and moral purpose

Children who come to a PRU can be volatile, angry, sulky, argumentative, defiant, oppositional and destructive, and they can swear a lot; they need to learn to conform to rules and boundaries and to self-regulate if they are to make a positive contribution to society. Often, children need adults to model the required behaviours. PSHE can also help to address issues children are facing in their daily lives, including expectations of conformity with social norms – for example, respect and other core values.

At the PRU we followed a values-based education (VBE) programme which was reinforced through assemblies, circle times and in class.[3] It focuses on emotional intelligence, which is vital to maintaining positive wellbeing in our children and young people. If mainstream schools are to successfully incorporate the needs of all pupils, they need to have a strong moral purpose at the heart of their ethos and demonstrate that all pupils are valued as individuals who have strengths and face difficulties.

PRUs are dedicated to finding the child behind the behaviour so that bridges can be built, leading to a better future. In order to do this we need to understand where the child is coming from, so in the next chapter I will look at the world from their perspective.

Notes

1 Camilla Turner, Children as Young as Four Showing Signs of Mental Health Problems, Teachers Say, *The Telegraph* (2 April 2018). Available at: https://www.telegraph.co.uk/education/2018/04/02/children-young-four-showing-signs-mental-health-problems-teachers/.
2 See https://www.teamteach.co.uk.
3 For full details see https://www.valuesbasededucation.com.

Chapter 5

The child: 'that kid'

So we've seen how things look from within the school and the PRU, but how does this all appear from the perspective of the child? I recently encountered a really inspiring parent, Claire Ryan, on Twitter, who was compelled to blog in response to seeing a tweet from a teacher, commenting "'Massive drain on teacher time is dealing with *That Kid*".[1]

I spent a long time considering how to try and fight *That Kid*'s corner, however with every idea came questions I'd like to ask that teacher. I decided that in order to try and change their opinions, I must first try and understand how and when they started seeing problems to be fixed rather than children to be supported [...]

He had already experienced years of disrupted education from being viewed as *That Kid*. His needs had been overlooked. His background hadn't been considered. Why had no one ever asked those questions? Never listened to his desperate mother? Never looked deeper than what they saw on the surface?

His story is one of disaffection, severe anxiety and needs which initially went undiagnosed. His mother was seen as one of 'those parents' and help was in short supply. Finally, after a long battle, the child did receive the help he needed. But as Claire rightly says:

'Dealing with *That Kid*' isn't an option to be considered. They need you more than the others and yes, they will take up more time and resources than others, but *That Kid* is just as valid as everyone else

---

and deserves a childhood free from unnecessary pain. If you have the power to help how can you even consider not looking past the challenges and seeing a child in need of support and understanding rather than *That Kid*?

Understanding 'that kid'

However, dealing with 'that kid' relies on emotional resilience and empathy, support within the school, an understanding of underlying SEN and how the child perceives the demands of the classroom, managing the reactions of other children and ensuring their safety, to name but a few. There is a whole web of complexity surrounding their needs, and of course this will also involve the needs of their peers and teachers. When I was at the PRU, I saw everything in black and white, but now from a mainstream perspective, I can recognise the grey areas that mitigate against full inclusion for some pupils. If a child has severe behavioural difficulties with underlying complex needs, including ADHD, ASC, PDA or attachment disorder, then exclusion might be the inevitable next step. But what if these had been diagnosed earlier in the early years foundation stage (EYFS) or Key Stage 1? What if schools had procedures in place for early identification? What if external agencies were better able to engage with children and families? There are so many what ifs.

These are questions that I hope will one day be the hypotheses of robust research rather than just my own musings. When I left the PRU in 2016, it was full of students with ADHD and ASC – and one of them was John, who I told you about in the preface. He was not 'naughty' but his behaviour was challenging due to sensory meltdowns associated with ASC.

Here is the transcript of our first discussion about his permanent exclusion:

Me:	You were permanently excluded from your mainstream school before coming here?
John:	Yes, I was.
Me:	And how did you feel?
John:	Sad.
Me:	Why were you sad?
John:	I didn't want to leave my friends ... And when I came on the taxi one time I got dropped off at my school and saw my teachers again ... I really miss them.
Me:	And were they pleased to see you again?
John:	Yes.
Me:	And had you always been at that school?
John:	Yes ... Not been to another school.
Me:	Did you go there in Reception or nursery?
John:	I think it was nursery up to Year 3.
Me:	And how did you feel when you came here [to the PRU]?
John:	Well, when I first came I was bullied because I was new ... I feel settled in now.
Me:	Would you like to go back to your mainstream school?
John:	Yes, so I could see my friends all the time.
Me:	Do you not see your friends at home?
John:	No, we don't play out at home.
Me:	But you feel settled in here now?
John:	Yes, I like it.

John was 8 years old at the time, and was able to articulate clearly how he felt. His words tell more of a story than any amount of dry research or facts and figures could; they come straight from the heart. As I mentioned in the preface, John wrote in my leaving book: 'hope you help children get back to mainstream school'. I am driven by this each and every day, it is even inscribed on the back of my business cards.

What are we doing to children with SEN? Yes, John had needs which were difficult to manage in school, but he should not have had to be permanently excluded before anyone found out what they were. He is placed in a special school, but why did he have to get there via a PRU? John now has a diagnosis of ASC and an EHCP to support him up to age 25; however, if he had been diagnosed appropriately in nursery he would not have had to undergo the separation anxiety he experienced in Year 3 when he was moved away from his teachers and friends.

Defending children's rights

We know from the 2018 Department for Education report that children with SEN are being excluded, even those with EHCPs, so there is obviously something wrong with the system.[2] As long ago as 2012, the Office of the Children's Commissioner produced a report on school exclusions entitled 'They Never Give up on You'.[3] The post of Children's Commissioner was established by the Children Act 2004, and under that act is required both to publish findings from talking and listening to children and young people – in particular those whose voices are least likely to be heard – and to engage with national policy-makers and agencies to inform policies and processes.[4] The work of the Children's Commissioner is underpinned by the UN Convention on the Rights of the Child (UNCRC), which is worth schools reading up on as it focuses on the rights and responsibilities which should be at the heart of inclusive practice.

The report identified the following rights as most relevant to policy relating to school exclusion:

- Article 2: All rights apply to all children regardless of their personal circumstances and regardless of what they have done.

- Article 3: The best interests of the child must be a primary consideration in all actions.

- Article 12: Every child has a right to express their views regarding all matters that affect them; and for these views to be taken seriously.

- Article 23: Children with a disability have a right to special care and support.

- Article 28: Every child has a right to an education [...]. Discipline in schools must respect children's human dignity.

- Article 29: Children's education must develop each child's personality, talents and abilities to the fullest.[5]

It is worth watching the YouTube video of the same name as the 2012 report.[6] It moves me to tears, as it highlights the malign effects of exclusion. There are some interesting findings in the report, which I feel have not been properly addressed during the intervening years – for example, inequities in exclusion from school to school.[7] This is still the case today: exclusions very much vary from one school to another, depending on levels of tolerance and the systems in place. Incidents of exclusion as a form of sanction for minor infringements – such as the wrong haircut, shoes or jewellery – continue to make the headlines, as we saw in Chapter 2.

Justifying exclusions

But what happens when children's behaviour does endanger others and their learning?

Of primary-aged schoolchildren, the Children's Commissioner's report says:

Many of those submitting evidence of this Inquiry, including teachers, head teachers, children and young people, academics and community groups, have requested the prohibition of permanent exclusions for primary school age children. In the view of these contributors, children under the age of 11 rarely, if ever, exhibit behaviour which would necessitate permanent exclusion.[8]

How many primary schools would agree with these findings? In my experience, children under 11 are capable of aggressive, destructive behaviour – I have seen trashed classrooms and children and adults who have been hurt by very young children; an adrenalin rush can give them greater strength than you would imagine them capable of. Children in the PRU often hurt staff, despite Team-Teach training which starts with staff pre-empting these behaviours. When calm, these children can form fantastic relationships based on trust, but this does not preclude them lashing out when they are in a heightened emotional state. Incidents of violence or attempted violence are a daily occurrence, even in settings where staff have specialist training in managing this. Therefore, I think it is rather disingenuous to suggest that mainstream schools should just be able to manage really distressing behaviours, without suitable facilities and trained staff. In June 2017, *The Guardian* reported on a survey by the GMB union:

More than half of school support staff have been attacked at work, according to research that suggests the problem is on the rise.[9]

The article went on to suggest that one contributing factor might be the rise in the number of children with SEN in the system. It is unsurprising that support staff are bearing the brunt of this, as it is often them who are left to deal with tricky behaviours. I wonder how many self-congratulatory 'inclusive' heads are patting themselves on the back for *not* excluding, at great cost to the health and wellbeing of front-line staff. I have seen this in my own work supporting mainstream schools and it cannot be allowed to continue. The solution? To look at children's underlying medical and SEMH needs at an early stage and investigate necessary adjustments. It may be necessary to have a reduced timetable whilst the child's needs are under investigation. Of course any interventions that impact on the child's full participation in the educational offering should be made with full consideration of the statutory guidelines and by following due process. As I have stated, informal 'time outs' are not acceptable.

I have had many encounters with paediatric services who can be quick to cite a child's 'behaviour' or 'parenting', when in reality there is something underlying which needs diagnosis. I have to be very persistent in getting medical help for children, but it is so important as lives can be ruined. As I keep reiterating, schools need help. It is no use castigating heads for excluding challenging children with complex needs, when managing them results in stress for the adults – as indicated in the *Guardian* article – and ultimately absence, sickness and resignation. It is also not doing any favours for the anxious pupil, who probably needs a small, nurturing setting in order to thrive.

Recently, a school asked me for advice for an EHCP application for a Year 1 pupil, who was really in distress; his screaming regularly echoed through the school and upset children and staff. His one-to-one support worker was about to quit. How is keeping him in this setting benefiting the child and those around him? From my observations, he needs specialist provision rather than additional support in a mainstream setting.

If all children had access to suitable provision, there would be no need for exclusions. Early diagnosis, appropriate placements, a move away from the test-centric culture and broadening the curriculum would ameliorate many of the issues facing children with SEMH issues and underlying medical needs. I encountered a young woman with ASC on Twitter, who had been to a special school, which gave her confidence to return to mainstream higher education. Having been told when she was young that she would never lead a 'normal' life or achieve anything, she had recently graduated from university. Aside from the sheer cruelty of such comments, it is heartening to see how appropriate provision can facilitate success; we can see how inclusion at all costs is not helping children either.

Listening to children's voices

I would like to finish this chapter by examining a more recent report from the Children's Commissioner.[10] *Children's Voices* mainly focuses on the experiences of secondary pupils under the age of 17, and is a cautionary tale of what can happen to children who are 'in the system' from an early age and do not have the protection of an EHCP. For the most part, pupils found being in a PRU, or other alternative provision, was a positive experience and they were able to function better in a small, nurturing environment; however, many had fears for the future. Their comments about their education so far included:

'I got expelled from X school 'cos I was a very bad girl, I used to get in trouble all the time so they kicked me out .... They said I either had to leave or I'd get expelled so I left .... I wanted to go back to X but they wouldn't take me back'.[11]

'I don't come to school, for a start and I always like ... muck around in class, and I'm with the wrong people ... and my writing is a mess, my reading's a mess, my spelling's a mess.'[12]

If there was any clearer indication of unmet language and communication needs, I could not find it. Global developmental delay, poor processing skills – these issues are rife in our schools. Imagine being that child, struggling on until 16 without help, and you have anger issues arising from that frustration, and possibly mental health or family issues; this is a classic path to exclusion. I have many sleepless nights worrying about all the children we, as a society, and in education in particular, are failing. Many young people in the report felt their life chances were already limited:

'A big business job, that's impossible for me to do, 'cos I wouldn't know the first thing about all this paper stuff and all that ... and I'd hate to do it even if I did ... that'd be impossible for me.'[13]

'I might not get a job when I'm older because of this school.'[14]

We need to rethink the status of alternative provision, which pupils perceive as impacting negatively on their life chances. We should rethink our approach to SEN and focus on early interventions so that children can have their needs met appropriately, have hope and not see themselves as heading for the scrapheap. This is why it is so important for schools to have better systems in place – so alternative provision becomes a place of last resort, not an inevitable destination.

Limiting life chances

A damning report from the Prison Reform Trust sought to research the prevalence of learning difficulties in the prison population. The findings on dyslexia were worrying:

> dyslexia is three to four times more common amongst offenders than amongst the general population, with an incidence of 14–31%. Probationers too have shown lower reading levels than the general population: the Stop Project (Shropshire Probation Service 1998) reported that 12% of offenders on probation were virtually unable to read, 29% had reading skills poor enough to affect seriously any employment opportunities, nearly a quarter (24%) could not complete their name, address, or personal details on a simple form, and a further 46% could not write simple text to a level acceptable to employers. Just under a third (31%) showed positive indicators of dyslexia.[15]

This is heartbreaking, and it's easy to see how these individuals would feel sidelined within society. The report identifies another at-risk group:

> One of the most prevalent vulnerable groups amongst offenders comprises those who do not have an intellectual disability as formally defined but who have much lower cognitive and adaptive abilities than do either the general population or the offending population.[16]

How many of us can recognise children in our settings who fit this criteria? Can we honestly say that we are doing enough to nurture these adaptive abilities? One final point really struck me:

School exclusions are common for young offenders generally, though exclusion may reduce the likelihood of any learning difficulties being identified.[17]

This is a frightening bind and I've seen it in practice. Children would regularly come to the PRU having been excluded, but with no diagnosis – just a label of 'naughty' or 'violent' child. We were able to recognise the underlying difficulties but as an education system we need to recognise these signs much earlier and do something to intervene. This could be achieved if schools took a more holistic approach and held multi-agency reviews at an early stage. The most inclusive schools I've seen have rigorous systems in place for monitoring the progress and wellbeing of their children, ensuring that they do not stay on the fringes. However, schools can't tackle the issue without the support and intervention of medical professionals and CAMHS.

Notes

1   Claire Ryan, *That Kid*, *The Life of a Colourful SEND Family* [blog] (28 May 2016). Available at: https://claireyr123.wordpress.com/2016/05/28/that-kid/.
2   Department for Education, Permanent and Fixed Term Exclusions in England: 2016 to 2017, pp. 6–7.
3   Children's Commissioner, *They Never Give up on You*.
4   See http://www.legislation.gov.uk/ukpga/2004/31/pdfs/ukpga_20040031_en.pdf.
5   Children's Commissioner, *They Never Give up on You*, p. 5.
6   Children's Commissioner, 'They Never Give up on You' – School Exclusions [video] (21 March 2012). Available at: https://www.youtube.com/watch?v=ycy_zp6PxQU.
7   Children's Commissioner, *They Never Give up on You*, p. 22.
8   Children's Commissioner, *They Never Give up on You*, p. 84.

9   Jamie Doward, Most School Support Staff Have Been Assaulted by Pupils, *The Guardian* (4 June 2017). Available at: https://www.theguardian.com/education/2017/jun/03/most-school-support-staff-assaulted-by-pupils-union-survey.

10 Children's Commissioner, *Children's Voices: A Review of Evidence on the Subjective Wellbeing of Children Excluded from School and in Alternative Provision in England* (London: Office of the Children's Commissioner, 2017). Available at: https://www.childrenscommissioner.gov.uk/publication/childrens-voices-the-wellbeing-of-children-excluded-from-schools-and-in-alternative-provision/.

11 Children's Commissioner, *Children's Voices*, p. 8.

12 Children's Commissioner, *Children's Voices*, p. 21.

13 Children's Commissioner, *Children's Voices*, p. 21.

14 Children's Commissioner, *Children's Voices*, p. 22.

15 Nancy Loucks, *No One Knows: Offenders with Learning Difficulties and Learning Disabilities – Review of Prevalence and Associated Needs* (London: Prison Reform Trust, 2007), p. 19.

16 Loucks, *No One Knows*, pp. 20–21.

17 Loucks, *No One Knows*, p. 9.

Chapter 6

The parents' view

Now we've considered the perspective of 'that kid', let's take a moment to consider their parents' view. An article in the Canadian publication *Today's Parent* chronicled the anxieties felt by the parents of a child with SEN.[1] From an early age, Connor struggled with social interaction and was prone to tantrums and aggressive behaviour. His parents felt that many teachers did not understand that their child's actions were the result of his disabilities rather than deliberate obstinacy. In fact, his mother has observed how the school's response actually compounded these issues:

> 'Almost the entire time he's been in school, the focus has been on his deficits,' says Jennifer. That's become a self-fulfilling prophecy—as Connor is seen as 'a bad kid,' the more his negative behaviour is exacerbated, at school and at home.

I was particularly drawn to the following quote, which, to me, sums up the attitudes of some professionals towards the parents of struggling pupils:

> The behaviour—the outbursts and the inattention—is often misunderstood as your child's moral failing or the result of your terrible parenting.

This is a view which I encountered every day whilst at the PRU, as I often do now in my work in mainstream schools. Parents feel that they are judged and blamed, particularly if professionals are quick to recommend a parenting course. This is great as a supportive measure – and is intended to give parents appropriate help in meeting their child's needs and an opportunity to meet other parents in the same situation – but you can see how this could imply a slight on your parenting. I have, over the years, liaised with paediatricians over children who exhibit signs of ADHD or ASC and are being extremely challenging in the school setting. Parenting is usually flagged up first but if schools persist and put together a letter of support then underlying causes are investigated more seriously.

Parental responsibility

If parents attend an initial medical appointment with an apparently calm child in tow, the absence of the stressors of school will give a false impression of their issues. Some parents find it hard to get their thoughts across when faced by a doctor and can contradict themselves. It is usually a good idea for parents to jot down some notes before the appointment, outlining the key points they want to raise. In some cases, schools have arranged for staff members or interpreters to support appointments and parents tend to welcome this help – it makes them feel that they are being listened to and valued. It demonstrates how school and home are working in partnership to address the child's needs. When this is not happening, parents begin to feel alienated; they withdraw from school, physically as well as emotionally. One mum I knew of started to deliberately avoid conversations with the teacher at home time, and if school rang her mobile she would switch it off. Fear is at the core of this: fear of yet another complaint, of exclusion, of what is going to happen next. And when the 'next' is permanent exclusion then their worst fears have come to pass.

Most parents, despite their own issues, just want the best for their children but often feel alienated by the system and struggle to cope with the fact that their child is violent, destructive or disruptive in the school setting. Unfortunately, some parts of wider society seek to condemn young children without knowing the full picture and, even worse, some parts of the education system do this too.

Parents can be accused of 'bad parenting' if they are seen to 'give in' to their child rather than maintaining strict rules and boundaries. We need to remember that these parents are struggling with challenging behaviour at home – swearing, spitting, shouting, wrecking, hitting – and will often 'give in' through sheer exhaustion, particularly if they have other children to care for. We are all only human, and being judgemental doesn't help anybody. Programmes such as Incredible Years can have a massive impact on parenting skills and are often signposted by professionals.[2] However, they can be hard to access, particularly for working parents, as they require several two-to-three-hour sessions over a number of weeks. In my experience, the parents who would benefit greatly often struggle to engage or attend.

A joint home–school approach can often work well, but this does not include punishing a child at home for something that has gone wrong at school. Any strategies need to be positive, consistent and, above all, doable. I have seen parents become overwhelmed when something seems too difficult or complicated. Simple works best – for example, encouraging appropriate behaviour with stickers, small rewards or favoured activities. This would work well in both a mainstream school and home setting.

Experiencing exclusion

Many of the press reports of children who, according to their parents, have been 'unfairly' excluded have a darker subtext than is first apparent. Newspapers often polarise opinions and when a child is excluded from school it is natural for parents to defend them and for a school to quote from legislation by saying they are deeply sorry but all procedures have been exhausted and that the safety of other staff and children is paramount. Parents I have worked with have said:

'Exclusion has become a way to get more help … My child shouldn't have to go through that.'

'School just wanted to get rid of him as they couldn't be bothered dealing with his behaviour.'

'He was excluded by school because they did not have the staff to cope with his behaviour. He is autistic.'

'I just got left with a child who was excluded and it was so unfair. I was expecting another baby and it made me ill.'

'The school knew of his problems but he still got punished. I feel really let down by them.'

'They've kicked him out and given up on him.'

The unifying theme for all these children is undiagnosed SEN, which was only identified once they came to the PRU, without exception. There were clear signs of undiagnosed difficulties, but that is how they remained. This is such a common picture across the board, it is no wonder exclusions are on the rise. The family reported on in the *Today's Parent* article are Canadian, so it's not just parents in the UK who are struggling to access appropriate help and support for their children's complex needs; again we need to look at why this is so.

Working together

Mainstream heads and teachers need to maintain a positive dialogue with parents so that relationships do not subsequently break down, as is often the case. If difficulties with a pupil arise, then school and home need to come together right away and be solution-focused. If a confrontational approach develops between all parties and positions harden then relationships can become fractured, often irreparably.

If a school has called me in for help with a child, I often meet with the parents – and I find this extremely beneficial because they offer valuable insights and often have strategies which work at home and can be transferred to the school setting. I recently met with the mother of a Year 8 pupil and she made me aware of a number of issues which the school were unfamiliar with, and this subsequently helped me to develop strategies which worked for the child and the school. It is often useful for an impartial 'outsider' to mediate between home and school, particularly if relationships have gotten off on the wrong foot for whatever reason. It is certainly worth schools bringing in a specialist in behaviour and SEN, either from the LEA or independent, to give a different perspective. I often wonder how many exclusions could have been avoided if the lines of communication were kept open at a much earlier stage when difficulties first started to manifest.

A parental view of the PRU

So what was the experience of parents with children at the PRU? Initially, parents were often angry and felt let down by mainstream schools, even whilst acknowledging that they understood the reasons for their children being permanently excluded. Some felt that schools had not done enough to help or just wanted to get rid of them. For others it was a relief that their child was now in a place that offered specialised help and support; it was often a relief for the child too. PRUs are, by their nature, small and nurturing, generally having several members of staff to a class of eight children. Relationships are key – more so given the nature of the children's often complex needs including unpredictable and challenging behaviours – and high staff-to-pupil ratios allow these to develop. Sometimes, just being in the PRU environment can positively impact on home life as anxieties are reduced and both the child and parents are less stressed.

Parents are used to being called in to mainstream schools for difficult conversations with pastoral staff, teachers and heads. At a PRU this can happen but usually any problems are dealt with without resorting to 'summoning' parents; in any case, geographically this is not always possible. PRUs are often a long way from children's homes, which is why the LEA arranges and funds transport in taxis and minibuses. Parents cannot just 'pop in' as they might to their local school, so TAF meetings are organised as appropriate, every few weeks. This is part of the Common Assessment Framework (CAF), which relevant professionals follow to identify and address the child's needs and progress.

On the whole, parents liked the structure provided by meetings and were relieved not to be dreading the end-of-day conversation or the phone call home. Conversely, they could feel frustrated by the distance and 'removed' from what was happening in school. To try to reduce this, parents were regularly invited in for events and performances and sometimes, funds and staff allowing, transport was provided for those who would otherwise not be able to attend. We had parents' meetings to discuss pupil progress, outside of the TAF process, and hosted parent support groups at regular intervals. We were always available at the end of a phone and home–school chat books would go home with the child each day to facilitate communication.

Getting a diagnosis and support

Parents are usually relieved if their child gets a diagnosis related to their unmet needs; not because they 'want' a label for their child, but because it means they are accessing the right help and support, both at school and at home, and this can open the door to help and funding from other services. The CAF process should facilitate access to commissioned services providing counselling for the child and family, support in the home, therapeutic activities, and access to mental health services, such as child psychology. CAMHS support is also available for families where there is a high level of mental health need, usually linked to self-harm and other extreme manifestations of mental health issues.

When I was at the PRU I undertook CAF champion training and went on to support local mainstream schools with the CAF process. So what exactly does this involve? If a professional working with a child has concerns about their progress, they can assess and review the child's needs through the CAF process. CAF is an assessment that can be used by practitioners across multiple agencies to help identify the needs of children, young people and families. During the CAF process, a family will have a nominated person or lead professional who will coordinate the plan of support and action, and will be the point of contact for questions or queries. The CAF plan is usually followed by TAF meetings. At these meetings the family will meet with professionals to see how they can all support the child. The child and their family may be asked to complete a one-page profile, signifying that everyone is working together in equal partnership. TAF meetings are held every few weeks and progress is reviewed over time. The CAF forms part of a school's graduated response under the SEND Code of Practice (which I will look at more closely in Chapter 7) and can be used as supporting evidence in an application for an EHCP. Some English counties use early help assessments (EHAs) instead of CAFs but the intention is the same. There are specific forms which gather information about:

- The child, their siblings, their parents and their place in the family (e.g. the youngest of three brothers).

- Home, background, wider family.

- School, achievements, difficulties, including SEMH.

- Parents' and child's aspirations, wishes for the future.

- Medical needs.

- Whether any services are already involved with the family.

- Whether any services need accessing to support the family.

Parents are often fearful of this process because records are kept and meetings minuted, which can be daunting; however, it is designed to help them and is a good way for them to be involved in regular discussion about their family's and child's needs. In some areas a CAF is required for an application for statutory assessment as it forms part of the graduated response. I am still finding that some schools and parents are not aware of the purpose of a CAF; used correctly it is an effective way of working collaboratively. I must stress, parental consent is vital and the family can nominate the lead professional; it is not a process to be done to the family and meetings should not be held without them.

Understanding the legalities

Independent support is available from the LEA for parents of children with SEN. They have extensive knowledge of the law and can guide parents through it every step of the way. There are other national bodies who can help, such as the registered charity Independent Parental Special Education Advice (IPSEA), who can provide impartial legal counsel.[3] Ambitious About Autism has a wealth of information for parents about the legal entitlements of children with ASC.[4] Special Needs Jungle offers a treasury of advice and is run by volunteer parents.[5] In one blog post, Renata Blower asks, 'Is there meaningful accountability for illegal exclusions?'[6] She shares the story of Zoe, a mother who has had to fight against her 15-year-old son's illegal exclusions. Jack was attending a mainstream school and had been diagnosed with ASC. Zoe says of his exclusions:

'I must stress that neither of these exclusions arose because my son broke school rules, but occurred after members of the teaching staff had treated Jack very inappropriately and not in accordance to Jack's needs as described in his ECHP.'

Blower concludes that:

> Their story highlights just how little accountability there is for those willing to break the law and disadvantage SEND children, and just how the current system fails parents who are fighting for their child's right to an education.

It is important for parents to understand their rights and know who to ask for help. Zoe's case is an extreme one but by no means uncommon, which is devastating in an era of SEND reform. LEAs have to publish information on their website and schools similarly have to publish their SEND policy. If they don't, then they are acting unlawfully – and IPSEA can challenge such unlawful practices on your behalf.

As I have said previously, primary schools tend to use so-called 'grey' exclusions believing they are 'helping' children, but just sending them home is evading – not dealing with – the issues, and parents have no power of appeal. I have heard similar horror stories to Zoe's where secondary school children with ASC have been denied a proper education because the school are struggling to meet their needs, just wanting to 'wash their hands' of them.

As I keep reiterating, if a school is struggling, they need help and they need to be proactive in approaching relevant professionals to access it. Zoe took her fight to every agency going, but the school should have been in her corner too. She says:

> 'Nobody should be above the law, if evidence is found that exclusions are being used illegally, then head teachers must be held accountable to stop this abuse which is denying children of their right to education and causing untold damage to families.'

Finally, I want to conclude this chapter with a checklist which may be useful for schools as well as parents; it is not exhaustive but covers the main areas of concern.

Parents' support checklist

- Your child is entitled to high quality teaching – so if you have any concerns about your child's progress, ask to see the teacher.

- If your child has an unmet need, speak to the school SENCO and ask what arrangements are being put in place to offer further help; a child placed on the SEN register will initially be on SEN support according to the SEND Code of Practice. Progress should be monitored, usually half-termly, via an individual education plan (IEP) or learning support plan which should have clear, measurable targets for small steps of achievement.

- If you feel that your child has an underlying medical condition, your GP can refer you to a paediatrician for assessment. The school can provide a supporting letter if they are in agreement; in some areas schools can refer children directly to the paediatric service with parental consent.

- If your child is struggling with behaviour, ask the school if there are any services which could provide support – for example, a local PRU or other early intervention service. At my PRU, the intervention team made a massive difference to schools, children and parents and were often successful in preventing exclusion.

- If you work together with the school to try out and maintain successful strategies, then your child will benefit from consistent and supportive parameters.

- Opening a CAF and having regular TAF meetings ensures that targeted help is provided. Often a CAF will be a gateway to commissioned services, free to the user.

- If your child's needs are complex, the school will ask an educational psychologist to come in and do an assessment; you will all then meet to discuss next steps.

- It may be decided that the school, with your consent, will make an application for statutory assessment towards an EHCP. Your LEA website should explain this process thoroughly.

- Parents can apply for an EHCP themselves but should discuss this with the school first. This was sometimes useful at the PRU if a child was excluded with undiagnosed complex needs and the school could provide very little evidence of a graduated response. Parents have a legal entitlement to ask the LEA for their child to be assessed and do not have to provide supporting evidence, although if they have any this is obviously helpful.

- If you need impartial support for your child's SEND, your LEA should provide details of their independent services, which are free to the user, on their website.

- If your child is excluded for a fixed period, the school should provide educational resources for them to access at home. If your child is permanently excluded, provision for continuing education should be made from the sixth day. Parents have the right to challenge permanent exclusion on appeal and this is made through the school's governing body, who can either uphold the exclusion or reinstate the child. The rules that schools have to follow are set out in guidance from the Department for Education.[7]

Notes

1   Rachel Giese, Is There a Better Way to Integrate Kids with Special Needs into Classrooms?, *Today's Parent* (12 April 2017). Available at: https://www. todaysparent.com/family/special-needs/is-there-a-better-way-to-integrate-kids-with-special-needs-into-classrooms/.
2   See http://www.incredibleyears.com/programs/parent/.
3   See https://www.ipsea.org.uk.
4   See https://www.ambitiousaboutautism.org.uk/understanding-autism/education.
5   See www.specialneedsjungle.com.
6   Renata Blower, Is There Meaningful Accountability for Illegal Exclusions?, *Special Needs Jungle* [blog] (20 November 2017). Available at: https:// specialneedsjungle.com/is-there-meaningful-accountability-for-illegal-exclusions/.
7   Department for Education, *Exclusion from Maintained Schools.*

Chapter 7

Behaviour or complex need?

In Chapter 3, I outlined some of the characteristics of inclusive schools, and integral to this was an understanding of SEND and early intervention. In this chapter, I am going to focus on strategies to manage challenging behaviour and prevent the sort of escalation that can ultimately lead to exclusions. I will use case studies to illustrate how and why these approaches work.

Accessing the right support promptly

When I am invited by schools to look at behaviour, it is important to be realistic and practical. My local LEA has a behaviour toolkit which goes through countless strategies for supporting children, and buried in its hundred pages is some excellent advice; however, that is the problem, it's impossible to find. Conscientious heads are asked to refer to this before seeking further help and support, but this is not your first instinct when you have a child or staff member in crisis. What they need is clear advice and simple, workable strategies to help at the earliest possible stage. Often, schools soldier on until events spiral out of control, and then exclusion becomes more likely.

In an attempt to regulate a centralised service which includes other alternative provision providers as well as PRUs, heads in some LEAs now have to put in referral paperwork before being able to even have a discussion about the support they need. This has resulted in a bureaucratic maze which can be difficult for schools to navigate. In fairness, a lot of really excellent work is being done by all concerned, and some funding is available to schools, but a lot can go wrong when schools have to wait weeks for support. Staffing and the sheer weight of school need creates backlogs in the paper system, but sometimes a timely word straight away could help prevent escalation and possibly exclusion.

Children presenting with behaviour problems often have underlying medical conditions and complex needs. If these are suspected, it is important to obtain a paediatric referral. This is not about trying to 'label' a child, but about getting the right help. A paediatrician is also the best person to refer the child on to other medical services, which can include occupational therapy (OT), speech and language therapy (SALT) and CAMHS. Any delays in growth and development can also be investigated.

Following statutory guidelines

Schools need to be aware of their statutory duties according to the SEND Code of Practice, which identifies four broad areas of SEND:

- communication and interaction
- cognition and learning
- social, emotional and mental health
- sensory and/or physical needs[1]

Many children with SEND have needs that intersect these areas, and the code makes it clear that:

> These four broad areas give an overview of the range of needs that should be planned for. The purpose of identification is to work out what action the school needs to take, not to fit a pupil into a category. In practice, individual children or young people often have needs that cut across all these areas and their needs may change over time. For instance speech, language and communication needs can also be a feature of a number of other areas of SEN, and children and young people with an Autistic Spectrum Disorder (ASD) may have needs across all areas, including particular sensory requirements. A detailed assessment of need should ensure that the full range of an individual's needs is identified, not simply the primary need. The support provided to an individual should always be based on a full understanding of their particular strengths and needs and seek to address them all using well-evidenced interventions targeted at their areas of difficulty and where necessary specialist equipment or software.[2]

In a busy classroom it can be an exhausting process to achieve all of the above, even with support from the senior leadership team (SLT). I am currently working with some challenging children with SEMH and other underlying needs who are supported by EHCPs. In one school, a dedicated, hard-working teacher is close to breakdown due to the number of struggling children concentrated in her class. Fortunately, extra nurture support is being provided, allowing the children to be taught in small groups, overseen by the deputy head. Hopefully this will give the children what they need and improve wellbeing for the teacher and the rest of the class, who were being seriously disrupted on a daily basis. There is a balance of needs to be considered and this school deserves credit for being solution-focused without resorting to exclusion or jeopardising the safety of, and relationships between, members of the school community.

Let's turn to each of these areas of need for a moment:

Communication and interaction

Children and young people with speech, language and communication needs (SLCN) have difficulty in communicating with others. This may be because they have difficulty saying what they want to, understanding what is being said to them or they do not understand or use social rules of communication. The profile for every child with SLCN is different and their needs may change over time. They may have difficulty with one, some or all of the different aspects of speech, language or social communication at different times of their lives.

Children and young people with ASD, including Asperger's Syndrome and Autism, are likely to have particular difficulties with social interaction. They may also experience difficulties with language, communication and imagination, which can impact on how they relate to others.[3]

Experience shows that getting children the right help and support with SLCN is very tricky; often due to a lack of specialists – for example, SALTs. Many schools I work with are paying privately for this, often using pupil premium funding. Most children at the PRU had SLCN needs, and statistics showing a prevalence of these difficulties in the prison population seem an alarming portent of their future, if help is not forthcoming.[4] We need to be asking our LEA SEND teams some hard questions about EHCPs and funding. It is no use the government highlighting schools' statutory responsibilities if they are not prepared to finance this. The schools I work in do amazing juggling acts with their budgets, but with the best will in the world, someone will lose out if there's not enough money to go around.

Cognition and learning

Support for learning difficulties may be required when children and young people learn at a slower pace than their peers, even with appropriate differentiation. Learning difficulties cover a wide range of needs, including moderate learning difficulties (MLD), severe learning difficulties (SLD), where children are likely to need support in all areas of the curriculum and associated difficulties with mobility and communication, through to profound and multiple learning difficulties (PMLD), where children are likely to have severe and complex learning difficulties as well as a physical disability or sensory impairment.

Specific learning difficulties (SpLD), affect one or more specific aspects of learning. This encompasses a range of conditions such as dyslexia, dyscalculia and dyspraxia.[5]

Cognition and learning difficulties often go unrecognised because children's complex needs are masked by their outward behaviours – such as sensory meltdowns, impulsivity and anxiety – particularly if they have ASC or ADHD. Many children on this scale will also have developmental delay, dyspraxia and SLCN; these need to be recognised, with interventions put in place at the earliest possible juncture. A child I recently referred to a paediatrician was not only diagnosed with ADHD but also with suspected dyspraxia and SALT needs. An educational psychologist identified an SpLD in reading, writing and maths, possibly dyscalculia. The child has recently been referred for an EHCP. Again, SENCOs and medical support services need the time and resources to carry out these referrals and investigations, something which they are sadly lacking at present. This needs to change, or nothing will change.

Social, emotional and mental health

Children and young people may experience a wide range of social and emotional difficulties which manifest themselves in many ways. These may include becoming withdrawn or isolated, as well as displaying challenging, disruptive or disturbing behaviour. These behaviours may reflect underlying mental health difficulties such as anxiety or depression, self-harming, substance misuse, eating disorders or physical symptoms that are medically unexplained. Other children and young people may have disorders such as attention deficit disorder, attention deficit hyperactive disorder or attachment disorder.

Schools and colleges should have clear processes to support children and young people, including how they will manage the effect of any disruptive behaviour so it does not adversely affect other pupils.[6]

How many schools miss the underlying needs behind the behaviour? To what extent can schools be expected to manage truly challenging behaviours? The point here, to me, is about the adverse affect on other pupils. If schools cannot see a positive way forward that balances everyone's needs, what then? It's an impossible bind. We need to see that difficult decisions are being made daily on exclusion, and that support is needed to prevent exclusions where possible. Mental health and wellbeing is a subject I will be exploring further in Chapter 9.

Sensory and/or physical needs

Some children and young people require special educational provision because they have a disability which prevents or hinders them from making use of the educational facilities generally provided. These difficulties can be age related and may fluctuate over time. Many children and young people with vision impairment (VI), hearing impairment

(HI) or a multi-sensory impairment (MSI) will require specialist support and/or equipment to access their learning or habilitation support.

Some children and young people with a physical disability (PD) require additional ongoing support to access all the opportunities available to their peers.[7]

In addition to making provision for children with difficulties related to, for example, vision and hearing, we also need to be aware of the sensory difficulties that children with ASC or ADHD may experience that would fall under this category of need. For example, many children with ASC are noise sensitive or have difficulties with food, in terms of textures and smells, which can be severely debilitating, yet these children can be routinely excluded without their needs being addressed. A child I am currently working with has a diagnosis of ADHD and is on medication; he is also being investigated by a paediatrician for ASC. I did a sensory profile for him with his parent and this highlighted a number of sensory issues. He has ear defenders to wear at play times, which were a flashpoint due to hypersensitivity to noise, and is allowed to take his shoes off in class as he is hyposensitive to touch and needs to feel the floor with his feet. John, mentioned in previous chapters, had meltdowns which were managed by making reasonable adjustments in school. They were not solely due to behaviour issues, although he could be very controlling and use his behaviour to get his own way. This is difficult for us all as it is hard to separate chosen from involuntary actions; often the two are so intertwined it is difficult to address properly.

The importance of early intervention

Many nurseries in my LEA are struggling to get appropriate support from outside agencies – for example, specialist teachers, educational psychologists and paediatricians. Children are starting in mainstream primaries with undiagnosed complex needs. The SEND Code of Practice is clear on the importance of early intervention. It states:

> It is particularly important in the early years that there is no delay in making any necessary special educational provision. Delay at this stage can give rise to learning difficulty and subsequently to loss of self-esteem, frustration in learning and to behaviour difficulties. Early action to address identified needs is critical to the future progress and improved outcomes that are essential in helping the child to prepare for adult life.[8]

I know of one 4-year-old who was permanently excluded from his mainstream primary school. This happened when I was working at the PRU but, unfortunately, we were only registered to take 5–11-year-olds. I contacted another mainstream school to see if they would facilitate a placement there. The head agreed and our PRU agreed to support him in a very structured integration process. The child initially seemed to settle, but then presented with the same challenging behaviours that had led to exclusion: throwing things, trashing the classroom and attacking other children and adults (including the PRU outreach worker). After meeting with representatives from the LEA it was agreed he would attend a Sure Start nursery part time. It was thought that he had separation anxiety as he knew that if he misbehaved his mum would come and take him home – a strategy that worked well at the school he was excluded from. This nurturing approach was successful and he had a very good relationship with his key worker;

however, the LEA could not find another mainstream school to take him as, after a short trial at a third school, it was obvious that he could not cope in that setting. Meanwhile, I facilitated a referral to a paediatrician to investigate possible medical needs, and aged 5 he received a diagnosis of ASC. He came to our PRU for a short period, received an EHCP and then moved on to specialist provision.

The point is that his early needs remained unmet for a long period of time. Assumptions were made about separation anxiety, but no one dug deeper and sought professional medical help. No child should have a permanent exclusion on their record before they are statutorily required to attend school. If he had been able to come to our PRU, what role models would he have seen in his older classmates? Unfortunately, this is not an isolated case but it does highlight the importance of proactively seeking help from the LEA SEND team.

I will now take a moment to explore a case study that illustrates the process of identifying a child's needs.

Joint planning for progress

Child A is a Year 8 pupil who has recently been diagnosed with ADHD and is on medication. He is presenting with significant difficulties in class across all subjects and his behaviours are forming an increasing barrier to learning. He is an able boy who is in the top sets, and the school are concerned that his current lack of engagement and progress may mean he will need to be moved down and will struggle to fulfil his potential.

I was asked to come and observe Child A to see what strategies could be put in place to help. I spoke to the assistant head of learning support, the head of year and the SENCO and learned that a number of measures had been put in place to support him but with limited success. Child A had been given some one-to-one in-class support, but did not engage with this as he felt it made him look 'different' to other pupils. His behaviours include shouting and shrieking, and being disengaged, defiant, argumentative and generally disruptive. He had run up 25 pages of behaviour incident reports in the last two months alone; I was given three to examine as a snapshot of his difficulties. Progress scores for all pupils are expected to be above 90% but his were at 51%. In the last week, Child A had spent two days out of five in the behaviour support unit, from which he has been excluded for disrupting the learning of other pupils. Child A likes being sent there, enjoying the quieter environment and increased adult support, and appears to be escalating his behaviours deliberately so this will happen. He needs to be integrated back into class as he is missing out on so many learning opportunities.

I then met with Child A's mum to get some family background and see whether he was showing difficulties in his home environment. She stated that his behaviours were much improved at home since he started on medication and that he is generally coping better with impulsivity and hyperactivity; however, he is displaying a range of other difficulties which are causing him to struggle. He initially had issues with his eating but he appears to have regained his appetite now. Child A displays high anxiety and worries about things which should not concern him – for example, is there enough electric in the house? He does not like change and displays obsessive traits – for instance, he refuses to wear new trainers, despite his old ones being 'wrecked'.

She states he shows some signs of obsessive compulsive disorder (OCD), such as opening and shutting his bedroom door six times every morning. He randomly shrieks at home and has tics, which his CAMHS consultant says is part of his ADHD. He constantly bangs walls and appears to have sensory issues, being hyposensitive to touch. He loves to fiddle with a ball of sticky tack and this helps him to stay calm during his medical appointments. He likes computer games and gaming with his friends. He likes to play football, although struggles to be part of a team, as working with others and following the rules of the game is a challenge.

He is often emotional, particularly when socially excluded, and will often repeat himself. Other relatives have suggested he might have ASC as well as ADHD; school can also see traits and suggest he would benefit from an assessment of his social and communication needs. His mum admitted that she had little knowledge of ADHD and would welcome support from outside agencies. I suggested she contact an ADHD advocacy group; in my local area, ADHD North West (based in Morecambe) provide close support for parents and advise on medication and useful strategies in the home.[9] There will be similar organisations in each region.

I then spoke to Child A about what he finds difficult in school and how we might address this. He admits that he finds it difficult to organise himself and struggles to bring the right equipment into school on the right days – for example, he says he cannot find his PE kit at home. He likes PE and once he finds his kit he wants to be able to stay in the lesson and not be sent out. Although he is good at maths, he finds his teacher too strict so will often 'play him up'. He has been sent to the behaviour support unit for refusing to change seats in class, but says that is because he was used to his original seat and did not want to be moved. He likes the unit because they break down tasks and instructions into small, manageable steps. He admits he easily becomes bored and is often sent out of class for excessive talking.

Child A and I discussed possible strategies to help him cope better in class. He struggles to see that his behaviour is in any way a problem and seeks to blame others. He wants to stay in the top sets and do well in his learning.

Together we agreed on a course of action:

- His mum would contact an ADHD group for support.

- She would also take a copy of his report to CAMHS and ask for an assessment of his social and communication needs in relation to ASC.

- The school would help Child A develop strategies to manage better in class.

- Child A would have a ball of sticky tack in lessons to help him concentrate on what the teacher is saying.

- Child A would need to attend the first part of a lesson but could then take his work to the head of year's office. He will be given a card with targets for increasing the amount of time he spends in class.

> Child A will also be given a target to reduce the number of referrals he has to the unit; a target-setting approach has worked for him in the past.
>
> The school were willing to listen to advice from professionals and insights from home, which has really helped to facilitate the right support for this pupil. Child A engaged well in these discussions and it was a real triumph of teamwork in which all parties were listened to and consulted. This case study really illustrates the points I raised in Chapters 3 and 6 about the importance of communicating and working in conjunction with families.

Assess, plan, do, review

The assess, plan, do, review cycle is integral to a graduated response, both in EYFS and school settings. The graduated response requires schools to:

- Assess the child's needs.

- Plan a course of action using SMART (specific, measurable, achievable, realistic, time-bound) targets which encompass small steps of progress.

If this is followed correctly, it should ensure that a child with SEND receives the right intervention from an early age. In my professional practice I'm occasionally called into schools where this evidently hasn't been the case.

Every child is entitled to high quality teaching, and the SEND Code of Practice is clear:

Teachers are responsible and accountable for the progress and development of the pupils in their class, including where pupils access support from teaching assistants or specialist staff.[10]

As I said at the start of this chapter, catering for each learner's needs in a busy classroom can be a challenge. But it is one that teachers are legislatively beholden to, so they need strategies to help. The following case study illustrates how a child's complex needs can be catered for.

Proactive interim interventions

Child B is a Year 2 pupil who is presenting with significant social, emotional and communication difficulties. He has had input from SALT and a paediatrician and is due to be reviewed by the paediatric service. His SALT assessments show a mild delay in language acquisition but he has been assessed as functional. However, he struggles to communicate other than at a very simple level; he cannot sequence four pictures or follow a three-part instruction. Child B has also had a full assessment by an educational psychologist and is operating on the first centile: at the lowest end of the cognitive scale of learning difficulties. He has found the transition to Year 2 and a more formal learning environment difficult. The school have provided opportunities for him to access continuous provision with a Year 1 class at times in order to meet his needs, but he requires the support of an adult as he will hurt the younger children for no apparent reason. He is energetic, boisterous and very unpredictable. He is restless and struggles to interact appropriately with other children, attacking his peers and older children indiscriminately. He is easily distracted in class and will disrupt the learning of others unless he has one-to-one support from an adult. He has 15 to 20 minutes of phonics and maths interventions from a specialist TA each afternoon. In class he is supported by his teacher and the class TA, but is very demanding and struggles to carry out even short activities independently.

Child B's teachers say he easily loses interest in lessons, particularly when more abstract concepts are being discussed, and without one-to-one support he becomes very disruptive. They feel he does not always mean to hurt others and often appears to not be in control of his actions. He can be very kind and likes to be part of his class and to have friends, but he struggles to interact in an appropriate manner. He finds sitting hard and likes to move about. He enjoys PE but often his behaviour spirals out of control and he starts being aggressive towards his peers. He needs to be constantly watched and will act inappropriately if adult attention is not focused on him. He is operating well below age-related expectations and needs a personalised curriculum with a mixture of adult-supported short activities and independent tasks which he can access at his own level.

Child B's behaviours are indicative of ADHD and are a barrier to his learning. He has significant developmental delay both in speech and behaviour and is awaiting further medical assessments. In the meantime he has no access to further one-to-one support, so school need practical strategies to use whilst his needs are being assessed.

Child B needs help to access the class more positively, particularly at times when he is struggling with the curriculum. Approaches I recommended included:

- Using a visual timetable so he knows what to expect in the day.

- Using cards to signal 'now' and 'next' activities.

- Having a box of activities close at hand so that he can have some choice and practise delaying gratification. For example, a short, focused activity with the class followed by one of his own choosing.

- Giving him a fidget toy for times when he is sitting listening with the class for an extended period. Appropriate use should be modelled.

- Creating a calming down space in the corner of the classroom and a workstation where he would not be easily distracted or distract others, personalised with his timetable, cards and activity box.

- Enabling access to a tablet with some colourful, engaging learning activities that he can do independently. ADHD-friendly apps could be accessed. ADDitude recommends games such as 'Captain's Log', which enhances concentration, self-control and working memory (for more recommendations, see their website).[11] There are cost implications, however, so consult your LEA SEND team for further advice about options and funding.

- Targeting activities towards improving working memory and cognitive skills.

- Taking five-minute breaks with an adult to give him a chance to engage in physical activity.

- Assigning older playtime buddies to model appropriate games with him.

- Allowing opportunities to dip in and out of physical activity in PE so he is not overstimulated and out of control.

When I next visited the school to help with EHCP paperwork, Child B had been diagnosed with ADHD and was on medication. He was a lot calmer and was getting extra adult support; the recommended strategies were in place and seemed to be working. The children in his class couldn't wait to tell me how good he was being and he was so proud of his work, as he was now able to access the curriculum, reading and writing in particular. It is a real joy see schools' persistence and fine-tuning of strategies succeeding in meeting a child's individual needs.

The SEND Code of Practice outlines the steps that should be taken to ensure a child's needs are met and sets out a framework for collating evidence and removing barriers to learning.

Assess

In identifying a child as needing SEN support the class or subject teacher, working with the SENCO, should carry out a clear analysis of the pupil's needs. This should draw on the teacher's assessment and experience of the pupil, their previous progress and attainment, as well as information from the school's core approach to pupil progress, attainment, and behaviour. It should also draw on other subject teachers' assessments where relevant, the individual's development in comparison to their peers and national data, the views and experience of parents, the pupil's own views and, if relevant, advice from external support services. Schools should take seriously any concerns raised by a parent. These should be recorded and compared to the setting's own assessment and information on how the pupil is developing.[12]

This is where the CAF comes into its own: regular updates are shared and next steps planned for using a multi-disciplinary approach. It is always helpful for schools to engage positively with parents through TAF meetings. This next case study illustrates the importance of parents and schools working in partnership.

Creating space to foster independence

Child C was having regular meltdowns and would violently attack his Reception class teacher, other adults and children. I was asked to help with next steps, and quickly recognised that the relationship between the school and home was at the heart of the problem. Child C's mum felt that he needed to be in specialist provision and the school felt that he was aware of this and 'playing up' more so that she would be called and he could go home. He was on a structured integration into the class, with time in school being gradually increased – this was not a grey exclusion. However, his behaviour got to the point where it was impossible for the school to calm him down – even his mum struggled! I had a meeting with her and she poured her heart out. She felt that the school was not listening to her concerns, but actually it seemed that her anxiety about her child was so great she wasn't able to hear what they were saying either. It was useful for me, as an outside SEMH specialist, to act as mediator and I was able to explain the steps needed to obtain an EHCP and outline some actions that they could agree on in the meantime. So, working together, we iden-tified a safe 'calming down' space Child C could go to first thing in the morning with his one-to-one support TA. Here his favoured activities would be ready to access. The move into his classroom would be structured in small increments of time and he could sit with a special friend to help him settle. There was also a corner he could retreat to when anxious, with a box of activities, a cushion and an egg timer, for limiting how long he spent there before rejoining the group. This gave him some independence, rather than being glued to the side of an adult, and ensured his teacher could provide high quality teaching for him to access, without disrupting the rest of the class.

One secondary school I work with holds informal assess meetings with parents, school personnel and pupils before coming up with an action plan. This works really well and often highlights unknown areas of need in a more relaxed way; parents and pupils open up slightly more than in a hierarchical formal setting. Also integral to the assess stage is to review progress regularly and consult other professionals as necessary.

Plan

The support and intervention provided should be selected to meet the outcomes identified for the pupil, based on reliable evidence of effectiveness, and should be provided by staff with sufficient skills and knowledge.[13]

Ideally, an educational psychologist and specialist teacher should provide a framework for next steps, but again there is a cost implication here. In my LEA there is a shortage of educational psychologists, and private practitioners are filling the gaps but at a great expense to school budgets. This means schools are having to 'choose' which children receive external support whilst others rely on in-house provision which may not be as specialised. In some schools, pupil premium money is being used to facilitate support, and outcomes of interventions are being carefully monitored. As I have said, limited resources will mean that some children lose out, despite the creativity of school leaders in trying to spread out their budgets. It is also essential to note that planned strategies must be shared with the parents and any staff working with the child, with all information recorded on the school's tracking system.

Do

The class or subject teacher should remain responsible for working with the child on a daily basis. Where the interventions involve group or one-to-one teaching away from the main class or subject teacher, they should still retain responsibility for the pupil. They should work closely with any teaching assistants or specialist staff involved, to plan and assess the impact of support and interventions and how they can be linked to classroom teaching. The SENCO should support the class or subject teacher in the further assessment of the child's particular strengths and weaknesses, in problem solving and advising on the effective implementation of support.[14]

Strategies should be clear, doable and measurable; they should be included on a pupil's IEP or learning plan. As I have already stressed, high quality teaching is vital to ensure that the child's needs are planned for and to prevent a child becoming 'velcroed' to a support assistant who is constantly at their side. This dependence can create further problems. I have seen some challenging behaviours come to the fore when a staff member is absent, as many pupils with complex needs respond adversely to change.

One way of achieving this is to carefully plan groupings so that the child is not always left with the same member of staff. When I was teaching in mainstream I would always plan time with children with SEN. I planned and evaluated strategies for managing behavioural difficulties myself, as the teacher should be leading support staff, not leaving this to them. This may feel onerous, and the current obsession with targets and pupil progress can negatively impact on teachers' time. However, by investing in the planning stage and meticulously considering the needs of all learners, you can achieve high quality provision for all.

Review

The effectiveness of the support and interventions and their impact on the pupil's progress should be reviewed in line with the agreed date.[15]

This stage of the process ensures that the outcomes are monitored. (This may be in the form of an evaluated IEP or learning plan.) Again, liaising with parents and other professionals is critical, as is revising interventions after measuring impact and planning next steps. TAF or other meetings are invaluable for bringing all parties together. This cycle is particularly important if a child has an EHCP, or one is being applied for.

Assessing complex needs: a practical checklist

I would like to round up this chapter by summarising the practical steps that mainstream schools can take to facilitate inclusion when a child presents with challenging behaviour:

■ Check for underlying medical conditions by facilitating a referral to the paediatric service.

■ Seek specialist help where appropriate.

■ Contact local services for further support.

■ Reduce anxiety in the child by providing personalised provision and learning opportunities as appropriate.

- Build up a relationship with the child and provide nurture, mentoring or buddying systems where needed.

- Be aware of the characteristics of SEND conditions and how to meet individual needs.

- Ensure that staff are trained and updated in SEND and behaviour policies.

- SEND and behaviour policies should be whole-school, consistent and fair. Zero tolerance is not an inclusive strategy and discriminates against children from certain backgrounds.

- Prioritise high quality teaching. TAs and learning mentors should support this process, not become 'velcroed' to a child and expected to be their sole educators.

- Foster a collaborative approach with home. Parents should be engaged with and respected as those who know their children best.

- Ensure all staff are supported and safe. No one should feel that they've been left on their own in a difficult situation, or have their safety put in jeopardy.

- Ensure that the SENCO is given sufficient time to do their job well; this never combines well with nearly full-time teaching.

- Keep good records and have systems in place for monitoring the graduated response; EHCP referrals rely on these.

This is not an exhaustive list but a school that follows these principles will not go far wrong. I'm now going to turn my attention to the more detailed signals that might suggest an underlying need.

Notes

1   Department for Education, *Special Educational Needs and Disabilities Code of Practice: 0 to 25 Years Statutory Guidance for Organisations Which Work with and Support Children and Young People Who Have Special Educational Needs or Disabilities*. Ref: DFE-00205-2013 (London: Department for Education, 2015). Available at: https://www.gov.uk/government/publications/send-code-of-practice-0-to-25, p. 85.

2   Department for Education, *Special Educational Needs and Disabilities Code of Practice,* p. 97.

3   Department for Education, *Special Educational Needs and Disabilities Code of Practice*, p. 97.

4   See Loucks, *No One Knows*.

5   Department for Education, *Special Educational Needs and Disabilities Code of Practice*, pp. 97–98.

6   Department for Education, *Special Educational Needs and Disabilities Code of Practice*, p. 98.

7   Department for Education, *Special Educational Needs and Disabilities Code of Practice*, p. 98.

8   Department for Education, *Special Educational Needs and Disabilities Code of Practice*, p. 86.

9   https://www.adhdnorthwest.org.uk.

10 Department for Education, *Special Educational Needs and Disabilities Code of Practice*, p. 99.

11 https://www.additudemag.com.

12 Department for Education, *Special Educational Needs and Disabilities Code of Practice*, p. 100.

13 Department for Education, *Special Educational Needs and Disabilities Code of Practice*, p. 101.

14 Department for Education, *Special Educational Needs and Disabilities Code of Practice*, p. 101.

15 Department for Education, *Special Educational Needs and Disabilities Code of Practice*, p. 102.

Chapter 8

Spotting the signs of underlying needs

So what should we be looking out for when trying to identify underlying needs? (The 'assess' part of the framework.) I am going to cover some of the more common areas which, if not identified at an early stage, could lead to exclusion, and I will signpost you to excellent organisations and practitioners with resources to provide further information. For a start, I can really recommend *Supporting Children with Special Educational Needs and Disabilities* by Cherryl Drabble.[1] Cherryl is a super teacher and friend who is assistant head at an outstanding special school and has an immense knowledge and expertise in all areas of SEND.

Speech, language and communication needs (SLCN)

Nasen, the special needs charity, held a leadership conference in 2016 on the theme of supporting pupils with SLCN. Wendy Lee, one of the presenters, noted that the risk of a child having these needs may be related to:[2]

- Gender: boys are over-represented relative to girls by 2.5:1.

- Birth season: summer-born children are 1.65 times more likely to have *identified* SLCN than those born in the autumn.

- Socio-economic factors: SLCN is 2.3 times greater for pupils entitled to FSM and those living in more deprived neighbourhoods.

What you might see

- Poor literacy.

- Poor behaviour.

- Poor self-esteem.

- Limited play.

- Limited social interaction.

- Poor working memory.

Evidenced and impactful intervention should follow a graduated approach, including:

- Communication-supportive classrooms: schools need to audit resources, strategies and materials.

- Targeted support: some children will need evidenced interventions.

- Specialist support: this is vital in my opinion as teachers need to have specific strategies that they can put in place using expert guidance.

The National Association of Professionals concerned with Language Impairment in Children (NAPLIC) is a charity which champions research into SLCN. Their website features a number of resources.[3]

The Communication Trust (TCT) is a coalition of over fifty not-for-profit organisations, working to support SLCN.[4] It has a wealth of resources for children, parents and professionals. At the end of 2017 the Department for Education announced it was withdrawing funding, placing the future of the organisation in jeopardy. At the time of writing, there is a campaign underway to stop this closure, and I hope by the time you read this the funding will have been reinstated. Schools need to have these sorts of resources to draw on.

Autistic spectrum condition (ASC)

In December 2012, the Department for Education published a research report looking at the interrelationship between SLCN and ASC, using their preferred term ASD. One of the statistics stated:

3% of seven year olds (Year 2) have been identified as having Speech, Language and Communication Needs (SLCN), whilst 0.8% have been identified as having Autism Spectrum Disorder (ASD).[5]

My concern is with the term 'identified', as, in my experience, many children go undiagnosed with either condition. At the PRU, many pupils presented with one or both of these disorders and it was down to us to get proper assessments so that appropriate strategies for helping these children could be embedded. Many of the children needed EHCPs and some moved on to specialist provision. In mainstream settings, I still see children who are struggling on without proper support. So what do we need to know about ASC in order to help children who might have the condition?

The National Autistic Society (NAS) define autism as:

> a lifelong, developmental disability that affects how a person communicates with and relates to other people, and how they experience the world around them.[6]

However, this can show itself in many different ways, and no two children with autism will present as exactly the same. This individuality poses a problem as not everyone will fit into a neat diagnostic box. I have supported some children, like John, who have challenging behaviours and sensory meltdowns and can very easily be labelled 'naughty' and I have worked with calm children who show some typical traits but may present few obvious difficulties in class. However, what they have in common is underlying anxiety and a difficulty in making sense of the world around them. Some children may have a higher risk factor for ASC:

- Boys are about four times more likely to develop ASC than girls, although there is evidence to suggest it is harder to 'spot' in girls.[7]

- Siblings/other relatives of child with ASC.[8] There is research to suggest that siblings and other relatives may go on to develop ASC or autism-like traits.

- Children with certain medical conditions have a higher than normal risk of ASC or autism-like symptoms. Examples include fragile X syndrome, which is a genetic condition.[9]

- There may be a connection between children born to older parents and ASC but more research is needed.[10]

It is clear that the number of diagnoses of ASC is rising, although it is not clear whether this is due to better detection and reporting, a real increase in the number of cases, or a mixture of both.[11] The climate of awareness-raising – due in part to social media and successful campaigns by relevant charities and parents' groups – may have had some effect. Parents, in particular, can be powerful advocates when it comes to investigating underlying needs in their children, as we saw in Chapter 6. The process of reaching an ASC diagnosis is complex, involving a multi-disciplinary approach from a number of professionals, including paediatricians and SALT.

What you might see

- The child may avoid eye contact, preferring to look down or away.

- The child may show very little facial expression; they find it difficult to show their emotions or may not feel emotions as others do. Many pupils I work with find this area difficult and often do not understand more subtle emotions, such as surprise or sympathy, nor can they recognise it in others.

- As a result of the above, the child can lack empathy and often self-awareness; they may seek to blame others when things go wrong or focus intently on their own needs.

- The child may have sensory issues around loud noises, food and touch, and may exhibit body signs such as hand flapping or rocking, which they use to soothe themselves. The child can be both hypo- and hypersensitive, either craving sensation or experiencing sensory overload.

- Many children exhibit extreme anxiety, particularly when their routines are disturbed and they are faced with unexpected change.

I'll explore the sorts of strategies that can help through the use of another case study.

Tailoring support for ASC

Child D is a Year 2 pupil who has significant medical and educational needs, and sensory differences. He has a diagnosis of ASC and requires one-to-one support from a TA to access a differentiated curriculum and personalised learning programme.

His sensory differences include toileting issues – he will only access toilets outside his home if he is wearing a pair of pull-up pants which he performs in once he is in a cubicle. He is extremely sensitive to noise and often wears ear defenders both in and out of class. He struggles with social communication, playing alongside rather than with his peers, and can be very solitary in the playground. He has pica and will chew pencils, leaves, rubbers and other objects which could be a choking hazard. Child D struggles to concentrate in class and is easily distracted by anything happening around him. He currently has full-time one-to-one support in the class and accesses a small nurture group with five other children two afternoons per week, supported by his TA. This is to build up his social skills, including turn-taking and conversation.

The impact so far has been limited due to Child D's dependence on adult support; however, the strategies are enabling him to make small steps in his progress. Now he needs to build up some independence. The nurture sessions are having a positive impact – he is enjoying the interactions with the rest of the group and is benefiting from circle time, discussing feelings in a safe environment. Child D is secure enough with his toileting to access the bathroom used by the class, although he still needs his pull-up pants. He has a positive relationship with his one-to-one TA but needs to be a little less reliant on adult support.

Child D would benefit from some further strategies to promote interaction and independence in the classroom, such as:

■ An independent workstation, personalised with Mr Men pictures (his favourite). He would also benefit from a visual timetable, 'now' and 'next' cards and a postbox in which he could place completed activities, to encourage independence. Used well, this adapted workstation would help him to be less distracted by others and become more independent.

- An activity box with independent activities linked to the curriculum.

- Activities to support his motor skill development – for example, handwriting patterns, colouring patterns, picture books, picture sequencing activities, word games, maths games, construction tasks and other practical apparatus.

- A sticker chart as a reward system. Ten stickers mean a small reward – perhaps Mr Men related. Parents could reinforce this at home to support the continuity between home and school.

- A safe chew toy to help him self-regulate his pica. I gave him a chewy blue car especially designed for children with SEND; it's non-toxic and durable. The understanding is that this will lessen his anxiety and desire to chew unsafe objects.

Child D responded well to these strategies and the school contacted me some weeks later to ask where to get another chewy car as it had had so much use he needed a new one. For a child with severe behavioural difficulties linked to ASC, creating a safe environment is essential in attempting to manage meltdowns linked to sensory overload.

In secondary schools, I have helped students to recognise their own triggers and together we have looked at possible safe spaces in their setting and analysed times they are becoming most anxious, which helps them to pre-empt difficult situations and use self-regulation techniques, such as deep breathing, using a card to leave the classroom or talking to a trusted adult or peer mentor. Some issues may be linked to subjects or the timetable and these can usually be resolved by staff if flagged up.

It must be stressed that every child with ASC is different and *all* the ones I have worked with have demonstrated that they can be funny, charming, friendly, empathetic, kind and chatty in various degrees. In the right environment, with good support and specialist help, every child has the ability to thrive and maximise their unique talents and potential.

For further practical help and support, I highly recommend my friend and colleague Lynn McCann, who has her own team of specialist teachers and is extremely well qualified in the field of ASC. She has written highly acclaimed guides for primary and secondary schools.[12] Lynn is also a NAS accredited trainer and has done some excellent work with educators on ASC and also mental health, more of which later. I do a lot of work on SEMH in mainstream settings in my specialist teacher guise and many of the children with these needs also have ASC. It is important that they have the chance to work on their social skills with a trusted adult, either one-to-one or as part of a small group, as this will enable them to learn or practise valuable interpersonal skills and increase their confidence.

Sensory processing disorder (SPD)

SPD can affect children with ASC but it is also a stand-alone disorder.[13] SPD is a neurophysiological condition in which the brain and nervous system have trouble processing or integrating stimulus. Sensory input – either from the environment or the body – is not detected or interpreted correctly and this leads either to hypersensitivity (overstimulation) or hyposensitivity (where the individual craves stimulation).

Children with SPD may have extreme reactions to external stimuli – I've spoken throughout about children suffering from sensory meltdowns.

What you might see

- The child may be hyposensitive or hypersensitive to touch, taste, feel, sight or sound.

- The child may exhibit behaviour problems.

- The child may find it hard to calm down after being upset.

- The child may be reluctant to eat certain foods due to texture or smell (I have seen this cause problems in the dining hall, as they can also be troubled by excessive noise).

- The child may either like to be dirty or show a fear of it.

- The child may be clumsy.

- The child may appear to be anxious.

If a child is either hyper- (shies away from) or hypo- (craves more) sensitive to stimulation then adjustments need to be made in the school setting. The case study of Child D highlights the need to consider sensory issues such as pica or sound sensitivity and explore strategies to meet those needs.

Developmental Pathways for Kids is an American child therapy organisation that has put together a useful checklist of sensory processing issues.[14] This is not about formal diagnosis – OT services will have the expertise to do this – but it is about looking at the triggers for certain behaviours and putting strategies in place to manage them.

Training is available from a range of providers, but I have had valuable input from the wonderful Becky Lyddon, who also provides fabulous workshops for parents.[15] Her immersive sessions contain installations that replicate the sensory experiences felt by a child with SPD. It is important that if SPD is suspected, a referral is made to a paediatrician and OT so that the child's needs are fully supported.

Attention deficit hyperactivity disorder (ADHD)

I have seen first-hand how ADHD, or attention deficit disorder (ADD), is a prominent factor in the exclusion of children from mainstream school. Despite an upturn in suspected cases, there is still a lack of understanding in schools about the condition, its diagnosis and how to manage the child's difficulties. A recent poll carried out by the ADHD Foundation on teachers' perceptions of ADHD found the following:

Most teachers encounter ADHD in their classroom, but knowledge and confidence about the condition is mixed

- 89% of teachers interviewed say they either teach or have previously taught students diagnosed with ADHD

- 19% feel fairly or very uninformed about ADHD

- 25% of teachers feel unconfident in being able to help students, who show signs of ADHD, access the appropriate services and support[16]

Teachers acknowledge the impact of ADHD on students, but many are not aware that ADHD is a real mental health condition

- 72% of teachers interviewed say that ADHD has a significant impact on pupils' life chances

- 21% of teachers disagree that ADHD is a mental health condition and 15% said they don't know

- 78% of teachers agree that ADHD may be used as a way for parents to justify their children's behaviour, with 28% strongly agreeing with this statement

68% of teachers believe that children or students with symptoms of ADHD perform worse at school[17]

It is quite staggering that there is still widespread ignorance about ADHD and that it is not perceived in some quarters to be a 'real' condition. The teachers polled would clearly benefit from better training in this area.

Certain factors seem to increase a child's risk of having ADHD:[18]

- A genetic link – likelihood is increased if parents or siblings have it.

- Certain environmental factors – for example, smoking during pregnancy.

- Biological determinants – for example, abnormalities in the prefrontal cortex of the brain.

In most, if not all, the families I have worked with, there does seem to be a genetic component; many adults only recognise it in themselves or other relatives when their child receives a diagnosis.

What you might see

- The child may be fidgety or tap their hands and feet.

- The child may have problems staying seated in the classroom or in other situations.

- The child may be on the go, in constant motion.

- The child may be running around or climbing in situations when it's not appropriate. (Often on walls, trees and fences!)

- The child may have trouble playing or doing an activity quietly.

- The child may talk too much.

- The child may blurt out answers, interrupting the questioner or other children trying to answer.

- The child may have difficulty waiting their turn.

- The child may interrupt others' conversations, games or activities.

This can lead to children struggling in the classroom and problems with behaviour – for example, anger management issues, aggression towards adults and other pupils, poor self-esteem and being prone to accidents and injuries.

It is vital that every child with suspected ADHD is referred to the paediatric service. If a child exhibits challenging behaviour including aggression and the destruction of property then the child may need to be trialled on medication. I have seen some marked improvements, in some cases life-changing, when a child gets the right treatment. One 9-year-old told his mum, 'the helicopter in my head has stopped spinning' and apologised for everything he had put her through; he had previously come within a whisker of permanent exclusion for violent behaviour.

Of course, there are many people who disagree with children being given drugs, but when you see how their lives are being ruined because they cannot control their impulsivity, which is worse? This is a medical condition that needs treatment, just like any other. I always say to parents, if your child had a broken arm you would not ignore it. Doctors monitor dosage and side effects very closely, so medication should not be ruled out without careful consideration.

Complex needs in a secondary setting

Child E is a Year 7 pupil who has significant SEMH needs which are presenting a barrier to his learning and to social relationships with adults and other children. He has a diagnosis of ASC and displays significant features of ADHD which are being investigated by CAMHS. Child E is cognitively high functioning but has difficulty processing oral information in his lessons. He responds well in subjects which have a practical element such as science and drama but can be disruptive in lessons he is not interested in or dislikes. His school have a behaviour policy whereby pupils are sent to the referral room after three verbal warnings. Child E is happy to be referred as he enjoys one-to-one time with the SENCO; he also uses this time to read, which he is passionate about – he would happily read all day if he was allowed. When debriefed on incidents, he is able to demonstrate an apparently rational response to what has happened. The SENCO brought in a sticker system with a reward of golden time in the last lesson of the day if he has earned enough stickers; he can choose to access the lesson instead if he so wishes. This system worked well initially but there has been a dip in behaviour and he has been in the referral room with increasing regularity.

Emotionally, Child E is operating at Reception level although intellectually he is well above age-related expectations. He appears to have attachment difficulties and developmental delay. His family have real concerns about his behaviour at home and are desperate for help. He has severe meltdowns – for example, over homework. The school have said that homework need not be completed at these times. He often complains that he has been bullied but does not perceive that he incites others by deliberately winding them up. He is extremely articulate but uses this ability to manipulate situations and people – for example, Child E was very clear in describing his difficulties and told me he was happy in school, yet his family report that he is always saying that he hates it.

Possible strategies:

- Child E needs help at the beginning of lessons as these often include direct instruction – this can be a trigger as he has poor oral processing skills and becomes disengaged and disruptive.

- Although he needs adult help this should be carefully scaffolded with independence built in.

- Short activities with visual cues will help him process information.

- He would benefit from a consistent approach with clear rules and boundaries which he can understand and follow. Tactical ignoring of low-level behaviour whilst praising others for desirable behaviours could help. Other pupils should be asked to withhold attention where possible – for example, by quietly asking to move seats if he's being distracting, rather than challenging him.

- Presenting a choice of activities which he can do independently may help pre-empt negative behaviours.

- Having the option to withdraw into a safe space – one TA said she had moved him to the back of the class when he became agitated and that this had helped.

It was clear that Child E had complex needs and required an EHCP to support these; however, practical strategies that take account of needs can make a real difference.

I would like to conclude this chapter by observing that many children have a combination of these disorders. Early intervention can halt the progress of challenging behaviours, and if a child really cannot cope in mainstream then there is time to apply for statutory assessment and seek the right provision before exclusion becomes necessary.

In the next chapter I will be looking at mental health and well-being and nurture provision; successful initiatives in schools can reduce the chance of exclusion significantly.

Notes

1   Cherryl Drabble, *Supporting Children with Special Educational Needs and Disabilities* (London: Bloomsbury, 2016). She can also be found on Twitter @cherrylkd.

2   Wendy Lee, Supporting Pupils with Speech, Language and Communication Needs, presentation given at the nasen Live Leadership Conference (7 April 2016). Available at: http://www.nasen.org.uk/utilities/download.400860AB-339A-44E7-8AE0FBECD723F141.html, p. 22.

3   https://www.naplic.org.uk/.

4   http://www.thecommunicationtrust.org.uk/.

5   Elena Meschi et al., *The Transitions between Categories of Special Educational Needs of Pupils with Speech, Language and Communication Needs (SLCN) and Autism Spectrum Disorder (ASD) as They Progress through the Education System*. Ref: DFE-RR247_BCRP11 27.12.12 (London: Department for Education, 2012). Available at: https://www.gov.uk/government/publications/the-transitions-between-categories-of-special-educational-needs-of-pupils-with-speech-language-and-communication-needs-slcn-and-autism-spectrum-dis, p. 4.

6   https://www.autism.org.uk/about/what-is.aspx.

7   https://www.autism.org.uk/about/what-is/gender.aspx.

8   Stelios Georgiades, Autism Predisposition among Children of Adult Siblings, *Autism Speaks* [blog] (30 November 2012). Available at: https://www.autismspeaks.org/expert-opinion/autism-predisposition-among-children-adult-siblings.

9   https://www.fragilex.org.uk.

10 Sarah Deweerdt, The Link Between Parental Age and Autism, Explained, *Spectrum News* (29 November 2017). Available at: https://www.spectrumnews.org/news/link-parental-age-autism-explained/.

11 Yasmin H. Neggers, Increasing Prevalence, Changes in Diagnostic Criteria, and Nutritional Risk Factors for Autism Spectrum Disorders, *ISRN Nutrition*, 2014, Article ID 514026 (2014). Available at: https://www.hindawi.com/journals/isrn/2014/514026/.

12 Lynn McCann, *How to Support Pupils with Autism Spectrum Condition in Primary Schools* (Accrington: Learning Development Aids, 2017), *How to Support Pupils with Autism Spectrum Condition in Secondary Schools* (Accrington: Learning Development Aids, 2017), *Stories that Explain: Social Stories for Children with Autism in Primary School* (Accrington: Learning Development Aids, 2018). Lynn can be found at https://www.reachoutasc.com.

13 See https://autismawarenesscentre.com/does-my-child-have-sensory-processing-disorder/ for more information.

14 http://www.developmentalpathways.com/services-sensory.html.

15 https://www.sensoryspectacle.co.uk or follow her on Twitter @Sensorysp.

16 Com Res, *Teacher Poll on Perceptions of ADHD: Findings* (London: MHP, 2017). Available at: https://www.adhdfoundation.org.uk/wp-content/uploads/2017/10/Teacher-Poll-on-ADHD-Findings-Oct-2018.pdf, p. 5.

17 Com Res, *Teacher Poll on Perceptions of ADHD*, p. 6.

18 See http://adhd-adduce.org/page/view/54/Risk+factors+and+causes+of+ADHD.

Chapter 9

Addressing mental health and wellbeing

The prevalence of mental health issues

So what are the statistics for child mental health issues? A report by the Children's Commissioner concluded:

Overall, 9.6% of children aged 5–16 have a mental health disorder, which is comprised of:

- 7.7% of children aged 5–10 having a mental health disorder

- 11.5% of children aged 11–16 having a mental health disorder[1]

The report is worth reading in full and gives a clear explanation of the tiered support system for treatment.

Unpicking this further, statistics from a 2015 report from the Department of Health reveal:

in an average class of 30 schoolchildren, 3 will suffer from a diagnosable mental health disorder.[2]

Common diagnostic categories are:

Conduct disorders: 5.8% or just over 510,000 children and young people have a conduct disorder.

Anxiety: 3.3% or about 290,000 children and young people have an anxiety disorder.

Depression: 0.9% or nearly 80,000 children and young people are seriously depressed.

Hyperkinetic disorder (severe ADHD): 1.5% or just over 132,000 children and young people have severe ADHD.[3]

This shows the scale of the work needed in schools to address the needs of a significant number of children; however, the situation may actually be worse as these numbers only represent those whose difficulties have been recognised.

Accessing the necessary support

The Children's Commissioner published a report in October 2017 on children's mental healthcare. In the foreword, Ann Longfield says:

At a time when the NHS is under exceptional financial pressure, the system in place makes it all too easy for children's mental health to be ignored. Nearly 60% of local areas are failing to meet NHS England's own benchmark for local area improvement.

The picture is even bleaker when it comes to early help for children with emerging problems. There is no clear expectation placed on local areas about which services should be provided, or how ill a child needs to be before they receive care. No information is collected on which local services are available, and the evidence that has been collected, by myself and a range of other bodies, reveals a postcode lottery of care.[4]

Following National Institute for Health and Care Excellence (NICE) guidelines, CAMHS follows a tiered model of intervention.[5] Tier 3 and 4 services are targeted towards children with the most severe difficulties. When asked how they determine whether to accept a referral, one tier 3 CAMHS in the North West told the Children's Commissioner they consider the following criteria:

- Severity: Is the problem at a level that is causing significant distress or disruption to the child/young person's life?

- Persistence: Is the problem ongoing and has not been resolved despite input from other services?

- Complexity: Is the problem made worse by other factors making change more difficult?

- Risk of secondary disability

- State of the child/young person's development

- Presence/absence of protective or risk factors

- Presence/absence of stressful social and cultural factors[6]

In my experience, CAMHS involvement is difficult to access; even if you feel that a child meets the criteria for intervention, the trouble lies with interpretation. I have known children who were gravely self-harming being dismissed as 'attention seekers' by both CAMHS and the child psychology service, who concluded that they would never actually kill themselves or try to. Even children admitted to hospital after self-harming were dismissed without further input. However, there are positive signs in my area as CAMHS are now coming into schools and talking to teachers and parents more often.

A report by the Children's Commissioner highlights just how hard it is to access services:

- On average, 28% children and young people referred to CAMHS were not allocated a service.

- 79% of CAMHS stated that they imposed restrictions and thresholds on children and young people accessing their services – meaning that unless their cases were sufficiently severe they were not able to access services.[7]

It is commonplace for both paediatric services and CAMHS to penalise patients for missed appointments, which is understandable in high-demand services; however, more could be done to check why. I know of one child who missed an appointment because their parent didn't speak English and so couldn't read the letter. The school had asked to be copied in but were not; fortunately, I was able to plead the case and a new appointment was scheduled, but what if there was no one to do this? Some schools lack the resources.

In 2015 the Department of Health published findings from a taskforce set up to promote, protect and improve children and young people's mental health and wellbeing. They identified the core requirements for improving the system as:

- Promoting resilience, prevention and early intervention

- Improving access to effective support – a system without tiers

- Care for the most vulnerable

- Accountability and transparency

Developing the workforce[8]

We certainly need change at a systems level. When I was at the PRU, I was actually part of the taskforce reporting on prevention and early intervention; this was a very intensive process as the timescales and deadlines were tight. However, mental health is something I am very passionate about, and I was anxious that the voice of the PRU was heard, particularly in relation to CAMHS access. The government ran a green paper consultation to consult on children and young people's mental health provision, the findings of which were released in July 2018.[9] There is a lot of detail and promise about forthcoming plans, but are any of them actually doable? Will enough funding be put in place? Are already overloaded schools and NHS services going to be able to cope with the extra demands placed upon them? We can only hope.

Mental Health First Aid (MHFA) England has launched a programme to train mental health leads in secondary schools to spot early signs and develop whole-school approaches to wellbeing.[10] Hopefully more and more schools will be able to access this kind of training.

Mike Armiger, a specialist teacher and consultant in trauma and mental health issues, has blogged about the importance of dialogue with pupils.[11] Of course, specialist support is necessary, but low-level conversations about feelings can really help too.

Mike clarifies how he sees teachers' responsibilities:

Are you expected to counsel someone through their depression? No.
Should we have to become experts in mental illness? No

Can we have conversations with a pupil about stress? Overwhelm?
Distress? Worry? YES.

Mike has some amazing suggestions about the types of language to use during these conversations, which I'd recommend reading in full. As he concludes:

It doesn't have to be scary. Shared language, in a school, in a community, is so powerful.

Together let's humanise mental health.

As I have found in all settings, building relationships, and a child knowing you have their back, can be a positive first step in supporting mental health. I only hope the government delivers in providing enough funding for services to work together effectively; it is very much needed.

Mental health is not just important for pupils

Before ending this chapter, I feel it is extremely important to talk about the wellbeing of staff. If staff are to provide good care for their pupils, it is important that their own needs are being met. Too often, teachers and support staff wear themselves out trying to manage challenging behaviours, and thus prevent exclusion, to the detriment of their own health. I know of one TA who was injured whilst supporting a violent child. She was not able to return to her post, but, tellingly, she did not blame the child at all, rather she said she felt unsupported by the head and SLT in being placed in that situation.

Writing in the *TES*, Will Hazell reports:

Tim O'Brien, visiting fellow in psychology and human development at University College London's Institute of Education, said the accountability system had left some teachers in a 'state of manic vigilance'.[12]

This sort of culture is risking teachers' own psychological health. On Twitter, I am proud to be part of a steering group who are campaigning to advance staff wellbeing.[13] Through blogging and Twitter we share healthy food ideas and recipes, and exercise and nutrition plans, with the aim of promoting self-care in the profession. This movement has a growing following and we have introduced a number of initiatives to encourage teachers to take better care of themselves and support each other.[14] It's also important to schedule time to talk with colleagues in school. Wellbeing really is a whole-school priority.

Notes

1 Children's Commissioner, *Briefing: Children's Mental Healthcare in England* (London: Office of the Children's Commissioner, 2017). Available at: https://www.childrenscommissioner.gov.uk/wp-content/uploads/2017/10/Childrens-Commissioner-for-England-Mental-Health-Briefing-1.1.pdf, p. 10.

2 Department of Health, *Future in Mind: Promoting, Protecting and Improving Our Children and Young People's Mental Health and Wellbeing*. NHS England Publication Gateway Ref. No 02939 (2015). Available at: https://www.gov.uk/government/publications/improving-mental-health-services-for-young-people, p. 25.

3 Department of Health, *Future in Mind*, p. 25.

4 Children's Commissioner, *Briefing*, p. 2.

5 For an example relating to depression, see https://www.nice.org.uk/guidance/cg28/chapter/1-recommendations.

6   Children's Commissioner, *Lightening Review: Access to Child and Adolescent Mental Health Services, May 2016* (London: Office of the Children's Commissioner, 2016). Available at: https://www.childrenscommissioner.gov.uk/wp-content/uploads/2017/06/Childrens-Commissioners-Mental-Health-Lightning-Review.pdf, p. 13.

7   Children's Commissioner, *Lightening Review*, p. 2.

8   Department of Health, *Future in Mind*, p. 13.

9   Department of Health and Social Care and Department for Education, Government Response to the Consultation on *Transforming Children and Young People's Mental Health Provision: a Green Paper* and Next Steps (July 2018). Available at: https://www.gov.uk/government/consultations/transforming-children-and-young-peoples-mental-health-provision-a-green-paper.

10   Caroline Hounsell, Upskilling Our School Staff to Support Pupils' Mental Health, *MHFA England* [blog] (27 June 2017). Available at: https://mhfaengland.org/mhfa-centre/blog/046119c9-125b-e711-8107-e0071b668081/.

11   Mike Armiger, Mental Health – A Shared Language, *Articulating Messy Thoughts* [blog] (7 January 2018). Available at: https://mikearmiger.wordpress.com/2018/01/07/mental-health-a-shared-language/.

12   Will Hazell, Teachers Suffering 'Fatigue' from 'Hyper-Accountability Industry', Wellbeing Expert Warns, *TES* (23 February 2018). Available at: https://www.tes.com/news/teachers-suffering-fatigue-hyper-accountability-industry-wellbeing-expert-warns.

13   Find us @HealthyToolkit and https://healthyteachertoolkit.wordpress.com/.

14   Search #SayYes2Wellbeing and #TeaAndTalk on Twitter for some inspiration.

Chapter 10

Holistic approaches

In this final chapter, I'm going to review a range of alternative approaches that I have seen schools employ to support children. These aren't necessarily classroom interventions, but can be used as part of a whole-school approach to pastoral care and behaviour management through self-awareness and self-regulation.

Nurture groups

A nurture approach offers a range of opportunities for children to engage with otherwise missing early nurturing experiences, giving them the social and emotional skills to do well at school, interact with their peers, and develop their resilience and capacity to deal more confidently with their lives. The Nurture Group Network (NGN) is a charity whose aim is to break cycles of low achievement. They say:

> The concept of nurture highlights the importance of social environments – who you're with, and not who you're born to – and its significant influence on social emotional skills, wellbeing and behaviour.[1]

The NGN outline six principles of nurture on their website:

1. Children's learning is understood developmentally

2. The classroom offers a safe base

3. The importance of nurture for the development of wellbeing

4. Language is a vital means of communication

5. All behaviour is communication

6. The importance of transition in children's lives[2]

There is a very useful guide which can be downloaded from their website, which describes the aims of a nurture group:

Nurture groups are an in-school, teacher-led psycho-social intervention of groups of less than 12 students that effectively replace missing or distorted early nurturing experiences for both children and young adults; they achieve this by immersing students in an accepting and warm environment which helps develop positive relationships with both teachers and peers.[3]

They report evidence of academic progress for pupils who have attended nurture groups. They are also key in developing and strengthening relationships and personal skills. The role of schools in promoting pupils' resilience is important, particularly for those with less supportive home lives. To set up a nurture group, a school would need a budget, willing members of staff to run it, and a suitable room. Some head teachers are using pupil premium funding for this. Nurture groups commonly use BOXALL profiles to measure the progress, both SEMH and academic, of children within the groups.[4]

Nurture group provision is about building positive relationships with pupils in which adults role model appropriate behaviours and social skills. Pupils are set goals using targets from their BOXALL profiles, and this focused and social work allows for cognitive restructuring. Often pupils learn to recognise anger triggers, and nurture provision can draw on concepts from affective education – for example, working with emotions and relaxation techniques, such as controlled breathing and mindfulness, more on which shortly. The NGN suggest that the theoretical model that underpins nurture groups stems from John Bowlby's attachment theory.[5] Essentially, the nurture group aims to be a surrogate for missing or distorted early social attachments.

In 2010 a documentary was made for Channel 4's *Dispatches* called 'The Nurture Room'. It was filmed in extremely deprived areas of Glasgow over a 12-month period and featured three schools with nurture room provision. You can see it on You-Tube.[6] It is extremely powerful and moving: I can really recommend watching it for an insight into this approach.

A PRU is not nurture group provision, but it is a nurturing environment and replicates many of the principles under-pinning the approach. Classes are small and staffed by consistent adults who build relationships with and secure the trust of very troubled, disaffected children, many of whom had so obviously missed out on early nurturing childhood experiences.

The Solihull Approach

I have been fortunate to access Solihull Approach train-ing, which was commissioned by our LEA a few years ago and given to schools and PRUs county-wide.[7] The aim is to increase children's emotional health and wellbeing through training for parents and practitioners. It combines three theoretical concepts from different strands of psychology: containment (from psychoanalytic theory), reciprocity (from child development) and behaviour management (from behav-iourism). It explores how different experiences surrounding attachment can impinge negatively as well as positively on how the brain develops, and examines reciprocity in develop-ing relationships with caregivers.

The idea of containment is an interesting one. It posits that if a person is 'full up' with their own worries and problems, they cannot effectively deal with the problems of others. This can be seen in families; a preoccupied parent may be 'full' of money worries, relationship issues and so on, leaving nothing to spare for the child. Professionals may become overloaded by the problems of families and children, on top of their own personal issues, until there is nothing left for them to give. This is why counsellors and other caring professionals have supervision – another adult to offload to – as part of their practice.

We tried to offer this approach at the PRU but it was so full on that there was often little time to move away from a stressful situation to reflect and 'contain'. It concerns me that if schools engage more in mental health first aid this could lead to issues with containment. We need to remember that staff wellbeing is also important. Perhaps teachers should have access to the more formal supervision procedures which are offered to counsellors to help them 'unload' their containment issues?

A real positive from the Solihull Approach is the ability to understand the issues children are facing and to know that nurturing adults have the power to reverse some of the damage done by poor early nurturing experiences. The brain really is remarkably malleable. In 2015 Frances E. Jensen, an American neurologist, conducted research following problems with her own teenage children. She wrote:

Parts of the brain connect to each other through synapses, which are insulated, just like electric wires. That insulation is a fatty substance called myelin, which is created over time. The process takes years, and it starts at the back of the brain and slowly moves forward. The last bits of the brain to connect are the frontal and prefrontal cortices, where insight, empathy and risk taking are controlled. This means that very smart adolescents will do very stupid things in a very impulsive way.[8]

I think it is important that we realise that the very wiring of a teenage brain can lead to risk-taking and impulsivity. Considered in conjunction with SEMH needs, it is no wonder that young people may behave in a way that will result in exclusion from school. I have seen this in numerous secondary settings and it is not going to improve without intervention and continued support being put in place. Many schools offer practices such as yoga and mindfulness in an effort to improve wellbeing. Schools need to be thinking outside the box in terms of helping students to develop self-calming skills.

Mindfulness

In essence, mindfulness allows you to catch negative thought patterns before they tip you into a downward spiral. It begins the process of putting you back in control of your life.[9]

Mindfulness focuses your thoughts 'in the moment' and helps you to cut out extraneous distractions, leading to a feeling of calm and control. So how can we use these principles to nurture children in our schools? Tammie Prince, a primary head teacher, has written a book full of ideas which are simple to implement.[10]

Schoolwell is a website run by Sam Collins, a teacher who passionately believes in wellbeing, and maintains a directory of resources for school staff.[11] She conducted an interview with Tammie in which Tammie revealed that she was attracted to mindfulness to counter the stresses of headship. She enjoyed yoga, but found the meditation at the end of the session the most relaxing. She realised that this could help staff and children too. Her top tips for teachers are:

▪ Develop your own mindfulness. A calm, Mindful teacher or leader will lead to calm and mindful children. When they see you being a good role model of Mindfulness, they begin to see the true impact of the lifelong skill. You will have better days and be happier. So will the children. Positivity begets positivity.

▪ Try out lots of ideas that you feel comfortable with and look at how it can be integrated into the daily life of your classroom. Transition periods are excellent times to insert Mindfulness activities. Get your children to "Stop and smell the roses!" Give them moments of peace. Develop it during periods of calm and encourage it in times of distress.

- Explain to children what is happening to their bodies during stressful situations and then explain the process of calming down. The more they understand this, the better they will understand the process and they will come up with their own ways to be mindful.

- A whole school approach to Mindfulness that runs through every aspect of the day, including assemblies, class work and behaviour management. Leaders need to be as mindful as the staff.

- Remember that stress is a part of life. We can't make the stress of the world go away. So, we need to learn how to minimise the effects of stress and not react in a way that enhances the stress.[12]

I find it extremely encouraging that some school leaders are working to create an ethos which is geared prominently towards promoting staff and pupil wellbeing, with a focus on robust support for the mental health of the school community. It shows that we *can* make a difference. I appreciate that schools are subject to intense external scrutiny but we can actively shape our own destinies.

Restorative justice

Restorative justice is very often misunderstood and can be thought of as a 'soft' process which seeks to 'excuse' the perpetrator and free them from the consequences of their actions. It is, in fact, a very powerful tool for promoting empathy and repentance, empowering the victim to have their say and often to suggest what consequences should be faced by the person who has harmed them. All parties must be willing to engage and resolution should be sought in a way which satisfies all those involved. Whilst at the PRU I undertook restorative justice training and went on to train primary schools in this approach. I feel that it has a really positive effect on behaviour and can play a part in reducing incidents in school.

An article in *The Guardian* reported on a campaign to introduce restorative justice to schools, against a backdrop of concerns about the rising number of exclusions:

---

amid what appears to be growing support for zero-tolerance regimes that punish pupils for minor breaches of regulations.[13]

I just wanted to quote this last point as it links back to the issue of tolerance that I raised in Chapter 3. Restorative justice holds harmers to account by getting them to take responsibility for their actions; it can be challenging to hear the person they have harmed sharing their thoughts and feelings directly. For victims, meeting the harmer can help them move on because they are able to say face-to-face how the incident has affected them. In the legal system, restorative justice conferences, where the two parties meet, are led by a facilitator who ensures that the process is fair. If a face-to-face meeting is deemed unsafe, the facilitator can use paper notes or video conferencing instead. Restorative justice in schools works in the same way as it does within the criminal justice system; the processes and procedures are the same.[14]

When I trained as a facilitator, the process was described as revolving around four key features:

1. Listening to other opinions and learning to value them.

2. Being responsible for your actions.

3. Developing an ability to repair harm.

4. Working through solution-focused processes.

Restorative justice originated in part from the practice of conferencing used by the Maori people in New Zealand and Aboriginal people in Australia. Peace circles are also used to resolve disputes in native communities in Canada and the US.[15] Howard Zehr directed the first victim–offender conferencing program in the US and has been called the grandfather of restorative justice. He has written many books on the subject and his *Little Book of Restorative Justice* is a bestseller which describes the fundamentals of the process.[16]

In a formal restorative justice conference, which can work well in a secondary school setting, the facilitator has to remain impartial and impassive; their role is to remain non-judgemental. The two parties are asked a set of scripted, guiding questions before the conference. The facilitator places the harmed person and their supporters on their right hand side and the harmer and their supporters on their left, forming a 'healing circle'. The harmed person is always brought into the conference first, to get settled. Ensure that they are not asked to wait together outside and that the venue is neutral. The harmed person is asked the questions first, then the harmer has their turn; the aim is to reach an agreement which is followed through. At the start of the conference, all parties are reminded of the ground rules and the aim is to keep everyone safe. Obviously there is the potential for things to become heated, so the facilitator needs to be alert at all times – in some cases a conference may need to be abandoned or postponed to give everyone a chance to calm down. More guidance can be found in the publication *Best Practice Guidance for Restorative Practice*.[17] The following questions may be helpful.

To the harmed person:

- What happened?
- What were you thinking about at the time?

- What have you thought about the incident since?

- How have you and others been affected?

- In what way?

- What do you think needs to be done to make things better/help you move on?

To the harmer:

- What happened?

- What were you thinking at the time?

- What have you thought about the incident since?

- Who was affected?

- How were they affected?

- What do you think you need to do to make things right?

These questions are carefully constructed in a way Zehr calls the 'paradigm shift'.[18] In schools, when children misbehave, it is common for adults to react by getting in the child's space and being accusatory; this has the effect of making the child defensive and can lead to confrontation, with both parties unwilling to give any ground. The child may become angry, resentful or stubborn and this may mean that negative incidents escalate quickly and spiral out of control. I remember just such an incident at the PRU when a child on respite was being reintegrated back into mainstream school. The child reacted badly to being shouted at by an adult and hit out: end of integration followed by a permanent exclusion. True, there needed to be consequences following the initial incident, but if the adult had modulated their response, the outcome could have been so different.

Restorative questioning takes the heat out of the situation as it is neutral, non-accusatory and gives all parties a chance to have their say. When children are in dispute, apportioning blame is rarely black and white. One boy in the PRU stabbed another child with a pencil and hurt him; however, it transpired that the other child – knowing the boy had a very short temper – was deliberately goading him for a reaction, which he got. This is not an excuse and the harmer did receive a fixed-term exclusion. An informal 'restorative chat' helped to resolve the situation and each party was able to show an understanding of why the incident had happened and committed to trying to get along better in the future; the harmer apologised and offered to shake hands, which was accepted.

Restorative chat follows a similar path to a formal restorative justice circle but is less time-consuming, and is therefore easier to manage in a busy school. I recently did some training in a school after the children asked the head for a way in which they could vocalise and debate concerns. Restorative questions were printed out on small cards, one for each of the adults in the school, including welfare staff. The aim was to provide a fair, consistent approach to minimise arguments and feelings of unfairness. A fantastic resource on YouTube is a video from Childs Hill Primary School showing restorative approaches in action.[19] It is vital that the concept permeates through the ethos of the school, otherwise it will not be effective.

Restorative chat fits very well into PSHE sessions and circle time. At the PRU we had circle time twice daily to address issues and problems, resolve conflict and develop positive relationships between the children. It aims to give them tools to engage with and listen to each other. As with restorative justice, there are ground rules for the circle. An object is passed around and only the person holding it can speak, encouraging respect, turn-taking and working together. Adults, as well as children, respond well to circle time: all participants are equal, visible and proactive. A circle is a powerful forum for a range of activities and discussions. There are a number of YouTube videos which show the power of circle times in a range of settings. One of my favourites is filmed in an American high school and shows how circles are used to create spaces for talking, sharing values, listening, encouraging empathy and resolving conflicts – a very powerful tool.[20]

To sum up then, a nurturing school that is actively trying to prevent exclusions will have a range of strategies available as part of its toolkit. Restorative justice, circle time, nurture provision and good PSHE all help a school to be more inclusive. However, these facets can never be 'bolted on'; they are integral to the life of the school.

Notes

1   https://www.nurtureuk.org/nurture/what-nurture.
2   https://www.nurtureuk.org/nurture/six-principles-nurture.
3   Nurture Group Network, *Nurture Groups* (London: The Nurture Group Network, 2017). Available at: https://www.nurtureuk.org/sites/default/files/ngn_-_nurture_groups-2017-05web.pdf, p. 2.
4   The profile, and further information, can be found at https://www.nurtureuk.org/introducing-nurture/boxall-profile-online.
5   Nurture Group Network, *Nurture Groups*, p. 12.
6   https://www.youtube.com/watch?v=5XFjLdNO4FU.
7   https://solihullapproachparenting.com/.
8   Frances E. Jensen with Amy Ellis Nutt, *The Teenage Brain: A Neuroscientist's Survival Guide to Raising Adolescents and Young Adults* (London: HarperThorsons, 2015), p. 24.
9   https://franticworld.com/what-is-mindfulness/.
10 Tammie Prince, *100 Ideas for Primary Teachers: Mindfulness in the Classroom* (London: Bloomsbury, 2017).
11 https://schoolwell.co.uk and Sam can be found on Twitter @samschoolstuff.
12 Schoolwell, Schoolwell Exclusive Interview with Tammie Prince, *Schoolwell* [blog] (29 October 2017). Available at: http://schoolwell.co.uk/exclusive-interview-tammie-prince/.
13 Sally Weale, Restorative Justice in UK Schools 'Could Help Reduce Exclusions', *The Guardian* (29 December 2017). Available

at: https://www.theguardian.com/education/2017/dec/29/
restorative-justice-uk-schools-help-reduce-exclusions.

14 For those seeking more information, Restorative Justice 4
    Schools is a leading provider of training and can be found at www.
    restorativejustice4schools.co.uk.

15 Elmar G. M. Weitekamp and Stephan Parmentier, Restorative Justice as
    Healing Justice: Looking Back to the Future of the Concept, *Restorative
    Justice*, 4(2) (2016): 141–147, DOI: 10.1080/20504721.2016.1197517.

16 Howard Zehr, *The Little Book of Restorative Justice* (Intercourse, PA: Good
    Books, 2002).

17 Restorative Justice Council, *Best Practice Guidance for Restorative
    Practice* (London: Restorative Justice Council, 2011). Available at: https://
    restorativejustice.org.uk/sites/default/files/resources/files/Best%20
    practice%20guidance%20for%20restorative%20practice%202011.pdf.

18 Howard Zehr, Justice Paradigm Shift? Values and Visions in the Reform
    Process, *Conflict Resolution Quarterly*, 12(3) (1995): 207–216. Available at:
    https://onlinelibrary.wiley.com/doi/pdf/10.1002/crq.3900120303.

19 Resolution Television, Childs Hill School and Restorative Approaches
    [video] (19 December 2011). Available at: https://www.youtube.com/
    watch?reload=9&v=AJWgayvuWXw.

20 Cassidy Friedman, Restorative Justice in Oaklands Schools: Tier One.
    Community Building Circle [video] (9 October 2012). Available at: https://www.
    youtube.com/watch?v=RdKhcQrLD1w.

Conclusion:
the journey so far and a
view towards the future

So what does the future hold for the children who are on the fringes? How can we use the experiences of the past and present to inform that future? How can we make changes for the better?

Speaking out and getting heard

It is heartening to see just how many practitioners, parents and supporters are acting as vocal advocates against the injustice of exclusions. Twitter has been a great platform to give ordinary teachers a voice, and many are also joining support groups, attending TeachMeets and generally becoming more informed about policies and practices. There are some great edu-chats taking place and some incredible specialists out there sharing their expertise for free. Some amazing grassroots movements are petitioning government and campaigning for greater transparency over exclusions.[1]

A particularly fascinating article in the *Evening Standard* describes how a group of South London students adapted a

Tube map visual to make a point. The campaign was seen by commuters, as stickers were placed on tube maps saying:

Every day, 35 students (a full classroom) are permanently excluded from school. Only 1 per cent of them will go on to get the five good GCSEs they need to succeed. It is the most disadvantaged children who are disproportionately punished by the system. We deserve better.[2]

This is amazing – young people are joining together to fight against unjust practices and yet this group are likely to experience at first hand the deleterious effects of excludable behaviours! I often wonder, if the children or young people concerned were also consulted, rather than adults deciding what is best for them, whether we might have a more rounded, compassionate view of those vulnerable pupils on the fringes. Of course, I am not talking about extreme behaviours or criminal conduct, but low-level behaviours that may make young people become susceptible to these in the future if they are excluded from school safety nets.

There is evidence that those in power are listening. At the time of writing, the findings of Edward Timpson's review into exclusions are awaited, following a pupil consultation.[3] Respected national school improvement leader Anita Kerwin-Nye commented:

… permanent exclusions are only part of the story. Timpson's review will be falling short if it fails to recognise and address the rise of implicit exclusion – the subtle and not so subtle messages that your child isn't welcome.[4]

When asked about this issue, Timpson's response was:

'It is totally unacceptable for schools to make themselves less welcoming for SEND students to improve their stats.'[5]

However, anecdotally, I have heard head teachers express concerns about their data when faced with an influx of pupils with SEND. I do not believe that they are uncaring but there is a lot of pressure on schools to perform well and evidence achievement, whilst Ofsted continues to be a worry. There is clearly a fault in the system as it stands. Anita concludes by saying that despite the constraints, many schools are managing to be inclusive and do their best for all their pupils; given the right support, many more schools will be able to achieve this. However, this exposes pupils to too much of a lottery of inclusion and we need a systemic overhaul.

Alternative models?

I have looked into examples from other countries to see if there are areas of existing good practice we can learn from; I have decided to use Scotland as a snapshot, given the dearth of evidence from other countries. Obviously there cannot be a like for like comparison given that England has a population of over 66 million and Scotland one of around 5 million. Interestingly, whilst Scotland allows permanent exclusions under severe circumstances, the system is completely different from that in England, where there were 7,720 permanent exclusions in 2016–2017.[6] An annual statistical report from Scotland shows a downward trend in exclusion since 2010, and in 2016–2017 only five pupils were removed from the school register.[7] This sounds amazing (even given the difference in population) so I had a closer look; surely if Scotland can virtually eradicate permanent exclusion, then there are lessons for all of us? The report states:

> Over 99 per cent of all exclusions are for a fixed period of time, referred to here as temporary exclusions, and pupils are expected to return to their original school when the exclusion period is completed.[8]

The characteristics of those pupils being excluded were pretty similar to those in England, with children more at risk according to:[9]

- Gender: overwhelmingly more males excluded.

- Additional needs: many excluded pupils had additional support needs.

- Deprivation: excluded pupils were typically more socially deprived.

I then looked at attendance figures, which were down for 2016–2017, and noted that children in areas of deprivation and/or with additional needs were more likely to have lower attendance than other groups; this was particularly prevalent in secondary and special school.[10] This needs further investigation as it is no use eradicating permanent exclusion if it leads to non-attendance in some cases.

Scottish schools do not have governing bodies as a rule, although some independent schools might; instead they have Parent Councils which are selected by other parents at the school.[11] In the case of exclusion it is the local authority who has the power to exclude, although this can be devolved to senior management in a school.[12] The criteria for exclusion is broadly in line with England but the difference appears to be that pupils stay on the school's roll, even if alternative provision is sought, and that there is an expectation that pupils will eventually return to their original school. In the meantime, they can be educated in another school, in another setting – for example, a library, or by another other means – for example, by telephone or email. (Remember only five pupils were removed from their school's roll in 2016–2017.) A Scottish source says there is no specialist provision for SEMH, such as PRUs or other alternative provision, and I cannot find any evidence that there is.

But what about provision for children with SEN? At first sight, Scottish education is extremely inclusive. Education Scotland's parent zone website states:

> All children and young people in Scotland have the right to be educated alongside their peers in mainstream schools, unless there are good reasons for not doing so.[13]

The website goes on to say that many mainstream schools are very successful in meeting the needs of all children – and that whilst some local authorities offer specialist settings as part of their provision, others have no special schools. Does this mean that schools are having to accommodate children with SEN regardless of their ability to meet their needs? The *Edinburgh Evening News* reported on a rise in the number of assaults on staff in primary schools.[14] In the same article, Educational Institute of Scotland (EIS) Edinburgh local association secretary Alison Murphy detailed how, at a recent AGM, members spoke at length about the problems of dealing with increasing numbers of young people with severe additional needs being placed into mainstream classes without proper support. If specialist SEN provision is patchy, it is inevitable that these kinds of problems will occur, and will ultimately have a significant impact on teacher recruitment and retention. Again, we can see the implications of inclusion at any cost.

In 2012 the Doran Report criticised the lack of national strategic services for children with complex additional support needs, and at the time of writing the situation is still the same.[15] A Scottish educator friend is currently concerned about a boy who is out of school for threatening others with a knife; unfortunately, in Scotland there is no youth justice provision. This friend told me that the presumption of mainstreaming is a disaster as it refuses to acknowledge the need for specialist input. There is no specialist provision in the LEA, so permanent exclusion is not an option – perhaps this is the real reason behind those low figures?

It is obvious that there are a lot of complex issues underlying the banner of 'inclusivity', but exclusion is not the answer either. We need a middle way. It is unreasonable to assume that the needs of all learners can be made to fit a one-size-fits-all model of provision and there should be a range of educational establishments, properly funded and scrutinised, tailored to individuals.

Looking to Europe and the rest of the world, there does not seem to be a model example out there that we can seek to emulate. We need to find our own tailored solutions. So, to conclude, here are my final suggestions for managing children with challenging behaviour in our schools.

A 10-point manifesto for preventing exclusion in primary and secondary schools

1. Prioritise the early identification of underlying medical needs. Schools and relevant health professionals need the time and resources to make referrals and applications.

2. The government should ensure seamless access to services, reducing bureaucracy and red tape around referral criteria.

3. Implement a streamlined multi-agency referral process, adequately funded, across the country which is binding for all LEAs.

4. Overhaul SEND and CAMHS services across the country, ensuring these are fit for purpose to provide help and support for schools, parents and children.

5. The government should provide adequate funding. Cuts are a false economy, leading to a future drain on services.

6. With increased resources should come a widespread mainstream school commitment to inclusivity and the recognition that individual needs should be met in these settings, except in exceptional cases.

7. An excluding school should have an obligation to continue to support the child, who will remain on roll for a period of time. However, this should be backed up by a commitment from the LEA to find a suitable alternative.

8. Suitable specialist and alternative provision should be available without cost to an individual school, for those children whose needs can't be catered for in mainstream.

9. Penalties should be in place for those schools that use exclusion to enhance exam results or as a zero-tolerance response for minor infringements – for example, over uniform, failure to complete homework and so on.

10. Reduce the emphasis on results and targets. Overhaul the one-size-fits-all curriculum which discriminates against those with SEND and the Ofsted accountability model which instils fear in schools.

As I said in the preface, thinking about the words of young John from the PRU keeps me focused on what is important in my work: 'hope you help children get back to mainstream school'. It is my hope that everyone reading this book will feel equipped and inspired to join me in the fight to ensure that no child is left on the fringes.

Notes

1   See, for example, @OnExclusions on Twitter.
2   Georgia Chambers, Powerful 'School to Prison' Tube Map Highlights Impact of Exclusion on Pupils, *Evening Standard* (23 August 2018). Available at: https://www.standard.co.uk/news/london/london-students-highlight-school-to-prison-line-on-gcse-results-day-a3918846.html.
3   https://consult.education.gov.uk/school-absence-and-exclusions-team/exclusions-review-call-for-evidence/.
4   Anita Kerwin-Nye, School Exclusion – The Story So Far, *Every Child Should ...* [blog] (14 March 2018). Available at: http://everychildshould.uk/school-exclusion-the-story-so-far/.
5   Quoted in Anita Kerwin-Nye, School Exclusion.
6   Department for Education, Permanent and Fixed Period Exclusions in England: 2016 to 2017, p. 3.
7   Scottish Government, Summary Statistics for Schools in Scotland No.8: 2017 Edition [A National Statistics Publication for Scotland] (12 December 2017, corrected 13 June 2018 and 5 December 2018). Available at: https://www.gov.scot/binaries/content/documents/govscot/

publications/statistics-publication/2017/12/summary-statistics-schools-scotland-8-2017-edition/documents/summary-statistics-schools-scotland/summary-statistics-schools-scotland/govscot%3Adocument, p. 27.

8   Scottish Government, Summary statistics for Schools in Scotland, p. 27.

9   Scottish Government, Summary statistics for Schools in Scotland, p. 28.

10   Scottish Government, Summary statistics for Schools in Scotland, p. 24.

11   For more information see https://education.gov.scot/parentzone/getting-involved/parent-councils.

12   https://www.autism.org.uk/about/in-education/exclusion/scotland.aspx.

13   https://education.gov.scot/parentzone/my-school/choosing-a-school/Special%20schools%20and%20units.

14   David Bol, Teaching Unions Call for Action as Edinburgh Assault Cases Soar, *Edinburgh Evening News* (12 April 2018). Available at: https://www.edinburghnews.scotsman.com/our-region/edinburgh/teaching-unions-call-for-action-as-edinburgh-assault-cases-soar-1-4722871.

15   Peter Doran, *The Right Help at the Right Time in the Right Place. Strategic Review of Learning Provision for Children and Young People with Complex Additional Support Needs* (Edinburgh: The Scottish Government, 2012). Available at: https://www.gov.scot/Publications/2012/11/7084, p. 11.

Bibliography

Armiger, Mike (2018). Mental Health – A Shared Language, *Articulating Messy Thoughts* [blog] (7 January). Available at: https://mikearmiger.wordpress.com/2018/01/07/mental-health-a-shared-language/.

Barkley, Russell A. (2000). *Taking Charge of ADHD: The Complete, Authoritative Guide for Parents*, rev edn (New York: The Guilford Press).

Blower, Renata (2017). Is There Meaningful Accountability for Illegal Exclusions?, *Special Needs Jungle* [blog] (20 November). Available at: https://specialneedsjungle.com/is-there-meaningful-accountability-for-illegal-exclusions/.

Bol, David (2018). Teaching Unions Call for Action as Edinburgh Assault Cases Soar, *Edinburgh Evening News* (12 April). Available at: https://www.edinburghnews.scotsman.com/our-region/edinburgh/teaching-unions-call-for-action-as-edinburgh-assault-cases-soar-1-4722871.

Brown, Brené (2010). The Power of Vulnerability [video], *TEDxHouston* (June). Available at: https://www.ted.com/talks/brene_brown_on_vulnerability?language=en.

Chambers, Georgia (2018). Powerful 'School to Prison' Tube Map Highlights Impact of Exclusion on Pupils, *Evening Standard* (23 August). Available at: https://www.standard.co.uk/news/london/london-students-highlight-school-to-prison-line-on-gcse-results-day-a3918846.html.

Children's Commissioner (2012). 'They Never Give up on You' – School Exclusions [video] (21 March). Available at: https://www.youtube.com/watch?v=ycy_zp6PxQU.

Children's Commissioner (2012). 'They Never Give up on You': *School Exclusions Inquiry* (London: Office of the Children's Commissioner). Available at: https://www.childrenscommissioner.gov.uk/wp-content/uploads/2017/07/They-never-give-up-on-you-final-report.pdf.

Children's Commissioner (2013). *'Always Someone Else's Problem': Office of the Children's Commissioner's Report on Illegal Exclusions* (London: Office of the Children's Commissioner). Available at: https://www.childrenscommissioner.gov.uk/wp-content/uploads/2017/07/Always_Someone_Elses_Problem.pdf.

Children's Commissioner (2016). *Lightening Review: Access to Child and Adolescent Mental Health Services, May 2016* (London: Office of the Children's Commissioner). Available at: https://www.childrenscommissioner.gov.uk/wp-content/uploads/2017/06/Childrens-Commissioners-Mental-Health-Lightning-Review.pdf.

Children's Commissioner (2017). *Briefing: Children's Mental Healthcare in England* (London: Office of the Children's Commissioner). Available at: https://www.childrenscommissioner.gov.uk/wp-content/uploads/2017/10/Childrens-Commissioner-for-England-Mental-Health-Briefing-1.1.pdf.

Children's Commissioner (2017). *Children's Voices: A Review of Evidence on the Subjective Wellbeing of Children Excluded from School and in Alternative Provision in England* (London: Office of the Children's Commissioner). Available at: https://www.childrenscommissioner.gov.uk/publication/childrens-voices-the-wellbeing-of-children-excluded-from-schools-and-in-alternative-provision/.

Com Res (2017). *Teacher Poll on Perceptions of ADHD: Findings* (London: MHP). Available at: https://www.adhdfoundation.org.uk/wp-content/uploads/2017/10/Teacher-Poll-on-ADHD-Findings-Oct-2018.pdf.

Department for Education (2015). *Special Educational Needs and Disabilities Code of Practice: 0 to 25 Years Statutory Guidance for Organisations Which Work with and Support Children and Young People Who Have Special Educational Needs or Disabilities.* Ref: DFE-00205-2013 (London: Department for Education). Available at: https://www.gov.uk/government/publications/send-code-of-practice-0-to-25.

Department for Education (2017). *Exclusion from Maintained Schools, Academies and Pupil Referral Units in England: Statutory Guidance for Those with Legal Responsibilities in Relation to*

Exclusion. Ref: DFE-00184-2017 (London: Department for Education). Available at: https://www.gov.uk/government/publications/school-exclusion.

Department for Education (2017). *Exclusion Guidance 2017: Government Consultation*. Launch date: 14 March (London: Department for Education). Available at: https://consult.education.gov.uk/school-absence-and-exclusions-team/statutory-exclusion-guidance/.

Department for Education (2017). *Exclusions from Maintained Schools, Academies and Pupil Referral Units in England: Government Consultation Response*. Ref: DFE-00183-2017 (London: Department for Education). Available at: http://dera.ioe.ac.uk/28702/11/Exclusion_Guidance_consultation_response.pdf.

Department for Education (2017). Permanent and Fixed Period Exclusions in England: 2015 to 2016. SFR 35/2017 (20 July). Available at: https://www.gov.uk/government/statistics/permanent-and-fixed-period-exclusions-in-england-2015-to-2016.

Department for Education (2018). Permanent and Fixed Period Exclusions in England: 2016 to 2017 (19 July). Available at: https://www.gov.uk/government/statistics/permanent-and-fixed-period-exclusions-in-england-2016-to-2017.

Department of Health (2015). *Future in Mind: Promoting, Protecting and Improving Our Children and Young People's Mental Health and Wellbeing*. NHS England Publication Gateway Ref. No 02939. Available at: https://www.gov.uk/government/publications/improving-mental-health-services-for-young-people.

Department of Health and Social Care and Department for Education (2018). Government Response to the Consultation on *Transforming Children and Young People's Mental Health Provision: a Green Paper* and Next Steps (July). Available at: https://www.gov.uk/government/consultations/transforming-children-and-young-peoples-mental-health-provision-a-green-paper.

Deweerdt, Sarah (2017). The Link between Parental Age and Autism, Explained, *Spectrum News* (29 November).

Available at: https://www.spectrumnews.org/news/
link-parental-age-autism-explained/.

Doran, Peter (2012). *The Right Help at the Right Time in the
Right Place. Strategic Review of Learning Provision for Children and
Young People with Complex Additional Support Needs* (Edinburgh:
The Scottish Government). Available at: https://www.gov.scot/
Publications/2012/11/7084.

Doward, Jamie (2017). Most School Support Staff Have
Been Assaulted by Pupils, *The Guardian* (4 June). Available
at: https://www.theguardian.com/education/2017/jun/03/
most-school-support-staff-assaulted-by-pupils-union-survey.

Drabble, Cherryl (2016). *Supporting Children with Special
Educational Needs and Disabilities* (London: Bloomsbury).

Dyson, Chris (2017). This is What Teachers Need: Smiles and
Love, *Integrity Coaching* [blog] (16 October). Available at: https://
www.integritycoaching.co.uk/blog/what-teachers-need.

Friedman, Cassidy (2012). Restorative Justice in Oaklands Schools:
Tier One. Community Building Circle [video] (9 October).
Available at: https://www.youtube.com/watch?v=RdKhcQrLD1w.

Georgiades, Stelios (2012). Autism Predisposition among
Children of Adult Siblings, *Autism Speaks* [blog] (30 November).
Available at: https://www.autismspeaks.org/expert-opinion/
autism-predisposition-among-children-adult-siblings.

Giese, Rachel (2017). Is There a Better Way to Integrate Kids with
Special Needs into Classrooms?, *Today's Parent* (12 April). Available
at: https://www.todaysparent.com/family/special-needs/is-there-a-
better-way-to-integrate-kids-with-special-needs-into-classrooms/.

Hazell, Will (2018). Teachers Suffering 'Fatigue' from 'Hyper-
Accountability Industry', Wellbeing Expert Warns, *TES*
(23 February). Available at: https://www.tes.com/news/
teachers-suffering-fatigue-hyper-accountability-industry-wellbeing-
expert-warns.

Holmes, Elizabeth (2017). More Smiles, Less Stick: Chris Dyson
on a Positive Approach to Behaviour, *Optimus Education* [blog]

(29 November). Available at: http://blog.optimus-education.com/more-smiles-less-stick-chris-dyson-positive-approach-behaviour.

Hounsell, Caroline (2017). Upskilling Our School Staff to Support Pupils' Mental Health, *MHFA England* [blog] (27 June). Available at: https://mhfaengland.org/mhfa-centre/blog/046119c9-125b-e711-8107-e0071b668081/.

Jensen, Frances E. with Amy Ellis Nutt (2015). *The Teenage Brain: A Neuroscientist's Survival Guide to Raising Adolescents and Young Adults* (London: HarperThorsons).

Kerwin-Nye, Anita (2018). School Exclusion – The Story So Far, *Every Child Should …* [blog] (14 March). Available at: http://everychildshould.uk/school-exclusion-the-story-so-far/.

Lee, Wendy (2016). Supporting Pupils with Speech, Language and Communication Needs, presentation given at the nasen Live Leadership Conference (7 April). Available at: http://www.nasen.org.uk/utilities/download.400860AB-339A-44E7-8AE0FBECD723F141.html

Leedham, Diane (2016). Nobody Puts EAL in the Corner, *Schools Week* (23 April). Available at: https://schoolsweek.co.uk/eal-learners-in-schools-how-the-government-could-help/.

Lindsay, Kali and James Rodger (2017). The Shoes Sparking Controversy at School Where 150 Pupils Have Been Put in Isolation, *Birmingham Mail* (7 September). Available at: https://www.birminghammail.co.uk/news/uk-news/shoes-sparking-controversy-school-150-13584251.

Loucks, Nancy (2007). *No One Knows: Offenders with Learning Difficulties and Learning Disabilities – Review of Prevalence and Associated Needs* (London: Prison Reform Trust).

McCann, Lynn (2017). *How to Support Pupils with Autism Spectrum Condition in Primary Schools* (Accrington: Learning Development Aids).

McCann, Lynn (2017). *How to Support Pupils with Autism Spectrum Condition in Secondary Schools* (Accrington: Learning Development Aids).

McCann, Lynn (2018). *Stories that Explain: Social Stories for Children with Autism in Primary School* (Accrington: Learning Development Aids).

Meschi, Elena, John Micklewright, Anna Vignoles and Geoff Lindsay (2012). *The Transitions between Categories of Special Educational Needs of Pupils with Speech, Language and Communication Needs (SLCN) and Autism Spectrum Disorder (ASD) as They Progress through the Education System.* Ref: DFE-RR247_BCRP11 27.12.12 (London: Department for Education). Available at: https://www.gov.uk/government/publications/the-transitions-between-categories-of-special-educational-needs-of-pupils-with-speech-language-and-communication-needs-slcn-and-autism-spectrum-dis.

Neggers, Yasmin H. (2014). Increasing Prevalence, Changes in Diagnostic Criteria, and Nutritional Risk Factors for Autism Spectrum Disorders, *ISRN Nutrition*, 2014, Article ID 514026. Available at: https://www.hindawi.com/journals/isrn/2014/514026/.

NEU (2018). Kevin Courtney, Joint General Secretary of the National Education Union, comments on plans announced today by Damian Hinds, the Secretary of State for Education [press release] (11 May). Available at: https://neu. org.uk/latest/school-places.

Nurture Group Network (2017). *Nurture Groups* (London: The Nurture Group Network). Available at: https://www.nurtureuk. org/sites/default/files/ngn_-_nurture_groups-2017-05web.pdf.

O'Brien, Jarlath (2016). *Don't Send Him in Tomorrow: Shining a Light on the Marginalised, Disenfranchised and Forgotten Children of Today's Schools* (Carmarthen: Independent Thinking Press).

Penfold, Mark (2016). *Improving Education Outcomes for Pupils from the New Roma Communities* (Leicester: EAL Nexus and the British Council). Available at: https://ealresources.bell-foundation. org.uk/sites/default/files/document-files/Improving%20education%20outcomes%20for%20Roma%20pupils.pdf.

Prince, Tammie (2017). *100 Ideas for Primary Teachers: Mindfulness in the Classroom* (London: Bloomsbury).

Resolution Television (2011). Childs Hill School and Restorative Approaches [video] (19 December). Available at: https://www.youtube.com/watch?reload=9&v=AJWgayvuWXw.

Restorative Justice Council (2011). *Best Practice Guidance for Restorative Practice* (London: Restorative Justice Council). Available at: https://restorativejustice.org.uk/sites/default/files/resources/files/Best%20practice%20guidance%20for%20restorative%20practice%202011.pdf.

Ryan, Claire (2016). *That Kid*, *The Life of a Colourful SEND Family* [blog] (28 May). Available at: https://claireyr123.wordpress.com/2016/05/28/that-kid/.

Schmoker, Michael J. (1996). *Results: The Key to Continuous School Improvement* (Alexandria, VA: Association for Supervision and Curriculum Development).

Schoolwell (2017). Schoolwell Exclusive Interview with Tammie Prince, *Schoolwell* [blog] (29 October). Available at: http://schoolwell.co.uk/exclusive-interview-tammie-prince/.

Scottish Government (2018). Summary Statistics for Schools in Scotland No.8: 2017 Edition [A National Statistics Publication for Scotland] (12 December 2017, corrected 13 June 2018 and 5 December 2018). Available at: https://www.gov.scot/binaries/content/documents/govscot/publications/statistics-publication/2017/12/summary-statistics-schools-scotland-8-2017-edition/documents/summary-statistics-schools-scotland/summary-statistics-schools-scotland/govscot%3Adocument.

Swann, Michael (chairman) (1985). *Education for All: Report of the Committee of Enquiry into the Education of Children from Ethnic Minority Groups* [Swann Report] (London: Her Majesty's Stationery Office). Available at: http://www.educationengland.org.uk/documents/swann/swann1985.html.

Tirraoro, Tania (2017). Ofsted and CQC Report on One Year of SEND Inspections. It Isn't Pretty, *Special Needs Jungle* [blog] (19 October). Available at: https://specialneedsjungle.com/ofsted-and-cqc-report-on-one-year-of-send-inspections-it-isnt-pretty/.

Turner, Camilla (2018). Children as Young as Four Showing Signs of Mental Health Problems, Teachers Say, *The Telegraph* (2 April). Available at: https://www.telegraph.co.uk/education/2018/04/02/children-young-four-showing-signs-mental-health-problems-teachers/.

Weale, Sally (2017). Restorative Justice in UK Schools 'Could Help Reduce Exclusions', *The Guardian* (29 December). Available at: https://www.theguardian.com/education/2017/dec/29/restorative-justice-uk-schools-help-reduce-exclusions.

Weale, Sally and Pamela Duncan (2017). Number of Children Expelled from English Schools Hits 35 a Day, *The Guardian* (20 July). Available at: https://www.theguardian.com/education/2017/jul/20/number-children-expelled-english-schools.

Weitekamp, Elmar G. M. and Stephan Parmentier (2016). Restorative Justice as Healing Justice: Looking Back to the Future of the Concept, *Restorative Justice*, 4(2): 141–147, DOI: 10.1080/20504721.2016.1197517.

Wheaton, Oliver (2017). Boy Ordered to Remove Sikh Jewellery or Face Exclusion, *Metro* (2 October). Available at: https://metro.co.uk/2017/10/02/boy-ordered-to-remove-sikh-jewellery-or-face-exclusion-6970656/.

Wilkin, Anne, Chris Derrington, Richard White, Kerry Martin, Brian Foster, Kay Kinder and Simon Rutt (2010). *Improving the Outcomes for Gypsy, Roma and Traveller Pupils: Final Report*, Research Report DFE-RR043 (London: Department for Education). Available at: https://www.gov.uk/government/publications/improving-the-outcomes-for-gypsy-roma-and-traveller-pupils-final-report.

Wolstenholme, Claire and Nick Hodge (2016). SEND Focus: 'Exclusion Affects Everyone – Pupils, Parents and Teachers', *TES* (14 June). Available at: https://www.tes.com/news/send-focus-exclusion-affects-everyone-pupils-parents-and-teachers.

Zehr, Howard (1995). Justice Paradigm Shift? Values and Visions in the Reform Process, *Conflict Resolution Quarterly*, 12(3): 207–216. Available at: https://onlinelibrary.wiley.com/doi/pdf/10.1002/crq.3900120303.

Zehr, Howard (2002). *The Little Book of Restorative Justice* (Intercourse, PA: Good Books).

The Little Book of the Autism Spectrum

Dr Samantha Todd

ISBN: 978-178135089-8

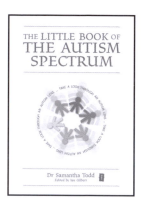

This teacher's guide will allow anyone who lives or works with children with challenging behaviour, behaviour problems, learning difficulties or on the autism spectrum to see the world as they do, and to develop strategies for managing and understanding autism effectively.

It peers through the 'Autism Lens', allowing us to understand autism effect change in terms of the way we deal with autism as a society and in education. It delivers evidence-based support and strategies that enable us to develop young people's abilities to interact with the social world, removing much of the anxiety that often accompanies it. An essential read for anyone working with children, and for young people on the autistic spectrum – and it will also prove to be a useful parents' guide to their child's mental health and emotional wellbeing.

The Little Book of Dyslexia

Both Sides of the Classroom

Joe Beech

ISBN: 978-178135010-2

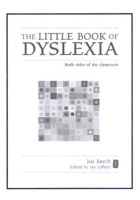

The Little Book of Dyslexia references both personal experience and current applied research and findings in order to highlight issues faced by people with dyslexia. It looks at a number of strategies and lesson ideas which can be used both inside and outside the classroom to help students with dyslexia and specific learning difficulties. It also lists various resources which can be used alongside these strategies to create a successful learning environment for those with dyslexia.

The Teacher's Guide to SEN

Natalie Packer

ISBN: 978-178583025-9

The Teacher's Guide to SEN details the areas of need teachers are most likely to encounter, including: speech, language and communication needs (SLCN); autism (or ASD); moderate learning difficulties (MLD); specific learning difficulties (SpLD), including dyslexia, dyspraxia and dyscalculia; social, emotional and mental health needs; and physical needs, including visual impairment (VI), hearing impairment (HI) and physical disability. It also provides a useful overview of the many potentially unfamiliar acronyms used in SEN.

Relevant to all primary and secondary practitioners, this is an essential point of reference for busy teachers, including trainees, NQTs or indeed any practitioner who would like to refresh their knowledge or gather some new ideas to try in the classroom.

The Perfect SENCO

Natalie Packer

ISBN: 978-178135104-8

Over recent years, the job of the Special Educational Needs Coordinator (SENCO) has become more strategic and will now include provision mapping, working in partnership with parents, supporting other colleagues, commissioning services, demonstrating pupil progress and ensuring value for money. In essence, it is a role which contributes significantly to whole-school improvement. *The Perfect SENCO* provides guidance for SENCOs and other senior leaders on working in a strategic way to support improvement. It will be of use not only for potential or newly appointed SENCOs, but also for those who are more experienced and wish to keep their day-to-day practice up to date.

Don't Send Him in Tomorrow

Shining a Light on the Marginalised, Disenfranchised and Forgotten Children of Today's Schools

Jarlath O'Brien

ISBN: 978-178135253-3

Jarlath shares some of the problems he's witnessed with inclusion and exclusion: mainstream schools actively encouraging children with SEND to look elsewhere, parents reporting their children have been formally or informally excluded from school and socially excluded by the parents of other children, children asked to leave their mainstream schools because of their behaviour – usually behaviour that is caused by their needs not being adequately addressed, children who are in school but isolated from their peers. If a child can't participate in activities or trips with the rest of the class, or spends much of the day working one-to-one with a teaching assistant, is this really inclusion?